WHAT MARTY BERGEN, AND OTHERS, ARE SAYING ABOUT *SECRETS*

"Cathy combines humor and insight as she shines light on a part of our bridge world that is seldom talked about. *Secrets* is informative and fun." **Marty Bergen**, Ten-Time National Champion, Author of *Points Schmoints!* and more.

"Cathy Hunsberger mixes her positive life philosophy with a delightfully humorous explanation of bridge intricacies and challenges. A fine feast." **Claudia McDonald**, ACBL Accredited Teacher, Journalist, ret.

"Cathy has been a bridge player for over 40 years. I have had the privilege of partnering with her in hundreds of games and tournaments at every level. In these pages, with humor and insight, she reveals the psychological aspect of this great and marvelous game of all games. Read and laugh." **Joyce Neville**, SLM and CEO, TAD Enterprises.

"This book is not just for bridge lovers. I don't play bridge but I found it amusing, entertaining, and full of the wisdom of life. My mother was crazy about bridge (her criteria for an assisted living facility was the quality of its bridge games). I have always been curious about the inner workings of the bridge circle, and enjoyed getting an insider's view of the fascination that takes hold." **Carol Chapman**, Author of *When We Were Gods*.

SECRETS YOUR BRIDGE FRIENDS

NEVER TELL YOU

The Silent Majority Speaks

Cathy Hunsberger

Illustrated by Bill Buttle

Honors Books is an imprint of Master Point Press.

Master Point Press
331 Douglas Ave.
Toronto, Ontario, Canada
M5M 1H2
(416) 781-0351
Email: info@masterpointpress.com
Websites: www.masterpointpress.com
            www.bridgeblogging.com
            www.masteringbridge.com
            www.ebooksbridge.com

Library and Archives Canada Cataloguing in Publication

Hunsberger, Cathy

Secrets your bridge friends never tell you
[electronic resource available] / Cathy Hunsberger ;
Bill Buttle, illustrator.

ISBN 978-1-55494-755-3

          1. Contract bridge. I. Buttle, Bill
II. Title.

GV1282.3.H85 2010
795.41'5   C2010-902168-1

THANK YOUS

My poor family did not even whimper when I locked myself away day after day in my home "office". They did knock hesitantly from time to time when it was the dinner hour...I love them.

My proofreaders and editors were constant and ever-ready. Carol Chapman, Claudia McDonald, and Joyce Neville gave me vital input and kept me straight for many months.

My mentor and illustrator Bill Buttle encouraged, advised, nagged, and threatened throughout. This project would not have gotten off the ground without him. He showed himself to be an unselfish professional with the courage to help an unknown get a start.

My bridge friends in Unit 110 contributed many strange and humorous stories from their life experiences. Among these were Chuck Sadowski, David Duhon, and Trish Richeson. Many others, reading articles I contributed to our Unit newsletter, urged me to get them into a book, and first planted that seed in my mind. Thank you all.

Brent Manley, Editor of the <u>Bridge Bulletin</u>, was the first to accept one of my articles for publication. He gave me the confidence to keep going, and while I know I was just one of many, I thank him for giving me a chance.

DEDICATION

This collection of thoughts and observations is dedicated to my bridge partner of many years, Joyce Neville, who suffered with me through many revisions, and missed games, during its progress.

CONTENTS

It's All About You!

When we first approach the bridge world we are offered an abundance of lessons on every possible technique. We learn to bid, to play the hand, to defend. We are taught rules and learn statistical odds. We are advised that a steady partner will help us advance. We go to tournaments in search of red, silver and gold masterpoints. We enter a world of magic and wonder and excitement.

Along the way, we begin to have doubts, we become unsure of ourselves. The experts and pros seem like giants towering over us. The director seems intent on monitoring our every move. We hear conflicting advice from all sides.

Am I going crazy, you may wonder? Is something wrong with me? Does everyone go through these unsettling experiences, or am I the only one? Will I ever make Life Master?

These are questions we don't hear much about, that are whispered in the corridors and never acknowledged. Rest assured, they are universal. In this small book we lay bare the journey of an individual as he starts his bumpy ride into the bridge world. He passes from fresh-faced beginner, graduates to intermediate, and finds advanced status within his reach. You may recognize part of your own journey. Most importantly, you will find you have never been alone.

Rest assured, all experts started as beginners. They just don't remember that far back.

THE MAGIC OF
SUCCESSFUL PARTNERSHIPS

"If we are together nothing is impossible. If we are divided all will fail." - Winston Churchill.

Bridge is a PARTNERSHIP GAME. This is the first tenet of bridge. It is the basis for all subsequent understandings, agreements and happy cohabitation at the bridge table.

Choosing a Partner
"Joint undertakings stand a better chance when they benefit both sides." - Euripides.

What should you look for in a partner? Ideally, you want someone you can be in sync with, whose mind set is similar to yours. You want a partner you can communicate with, argue with, laugh with, and in the end, start over with.

How does your mind work? Do you like a bid to mean the same thing every time? Are you very literal? Very creative? Do you like to experiment? These are factors that should influence how you choose your partners, how you approach the game, how you complete your convention card; these factors are often overlooked.

If you want a simple game, a light hobby, a straight-forward convention card, you are not going to be happy with someone who takes the game very seriously, wants to try any and all conventions, and analyzes each deal to the nth degree.

Know yourself and choose your partners wisely.

Choosing a System
"*Interdependency requires lavish*
communication." *- Max Dupree.*

You and your new partner must decide on
and learn the language with which you are going
to communicate. Go over your convention card
thoroughly. Ask questions.

Which *are* the best conventions? They are
the ones that suit you, your personality, your
game, your approach to the game. They are the
ones you and your partner agree on, and DISCUSS
THOROUGHLY.

There are an amazing number of ways to
play every convention. Don't just ask, "Do you
play Gerber?" Once you agree to play Gerber
ask your partner *how* he plays Gerber. Does he
play straight Gerber, does he play it only over
NT, does he play 1430 mini-maxi Gerber, etc.
Almost all partnership misunderstandings arise
from lack of thorough discussion.

Remember too, you are creating a unified
system, something that works and flows
together, that meshes. Check for duplications.
Do you have two bids for the same hand type?

Does the card seem more than you can
handle right now? Too much too soon is a
common source of misunderstanding and friction.
You want partnership rapport, not necessarily
every convention in the book.

Keeping a Partner
"*One beam alone, no matter how stout, cannot
support a house.*" *- Chinese Proverb.*

One factor that should remain constant is
flexibility. A convention card is only a piece
of paper. A system is not written in concrete.
It can be amended, changed, modified. It can
be screwed up in a ball and thrown away.

If a system or convention isn't working for you and your partner, change it, try something new, experiment. Ask an expert, read a book, take lessons.

If you are a serious student of the game, keep a log with all your bidding agreements. Upgrade it regularly. Go over it with your partner at least once a month. Constant memory enhancement helps reduce misunderstandings. Ask if you are <u>both</u> happy with this system. A happy partner is one of the keys to success.

Misunderstandings
"Do not speak - unless it improves on silence."
- Buddhist saying.

And finally, when misunderstandings do occur - as they inevitably will - keep calm and cool. Ask yourself what you would want your partner to say to you if you had just made that same stupid bid. After all, you both have the same goal in mind. These misunderstandings can be good learning tools and engender illuminating discussions. A "bad" bid can lead to bigger and better things. You may even thank your partner for his or her mistake!

End Result
"Success is not a destination, it's a journey."
- Zig Ziglar.

So, partners, discuss your goals, learn your own special bridge language. Be flexible and open-minded. Use your misunderstandings to lead to even greater understandings. You will have a fun time at the bridge table, with ever increasing success.

"Bridge is a partnership game." - Don Harrison (my first bridge teacher).

* * *

THE SEARCH

"Seek, and you shall find..." - Luke 11:9.

This is a true story. It unfolded as written, although you may shake your head in disbelief. Afterward, I recognized this experience might have bridge relevance as well. You must judge for yourself.

Have you ever taken a teenager out looking for a cheap car? It can be quite an adventure. In fact being in a teenager's company for any length of time can, in itself, be quite an adventure. One fine summer's day my then teenage son Stephen and I set out on such a search.

Our first tip was on a truck being offered by "Sam," a sweet man of 80-some years. He explained over the phone that he bought older vehicles and restored them, for something to do, and for a bit of extra cash. He assured us this was a great deal. He directed us to a used car lot on the side of the highway, where the owner allowed Sam to park his bargains. We arrived with high expectations ... which were squelched entirely at first glance. Stephen stood staring mutely, finally glancing at me with evident despair, while Sam rattled on about the truck's virtues. We both knew with certainty that at any speed over 35 mph this beauty would fall apart bolt by bolt. That is, if the tires didn't burst first. Or it didn't rust away before we even got started. Sensing our hesitation, Sam urged us, with a hopeful air, to drive the truck. He didn't propose we drive it on the road, but there was a graveled space behind the car lot that would do nicely, he suggested. More to make him happy than anything else, Stephen drove the car in circles around the field. Stephen then confessed that he just didn't feel comfortable with a shift, and we left Sam looking a bit deflated. Like the tires. However, I'm sure he soon perked up, and went on to putter with his next bargain.

We approached the next prospect with somewhat dampened enthusiasm. We met the owner at his farm, and hopped on his dune buggy to bump out to the south 40 where the car was abandoned, uh, I mean parked. The car looked fairly decent at first glance, paint intact, no rust – dare we hope? Then we opened the driver's door. There were wires running everywhere, in every direction, some not seemingly connected to anything. Getting gingerly in, Stephen suddenly jumped convulsively. "That wire's hot!" he yelped. Not exactly comforting. The owner then admitted that the car did need a little work (an understatement). He helpfully offered to let Stephen work on it there at the farm. He showed us a large concrete apron in front of a major tool shed. A tool shed that was crammed from stem to stern with every kind of miscellaneous tool and part imaginable. Unfortunately, there was no organization, just massive piles and heaps everywhere. As we moved rapidly away, mumbling about wanting to see a few more offerings before making a decision, Stephen eyed the owner's daughter. Now that, he commented, was *really* hot. Stephen conceded he might need to come back for a second look or two at the car after all.

A new day dawned. Next on the list was a Cadillac, described as a real jewel. We ventured out with extreme caution. We had both put in a day's work; it was viciously hot. The site was in a wooded area - mosquitoes swarmed, clouding the air. As we wound up the drive, we were totally unprepared for what met our eyes. A rich assortment of cars, trucks and vans of every description and condition filled the yard. A young woman, looking rather at sea, stepped out of her mobile home to greet us. We had spotted a likely van parked a few cars back from the Cadillac, and asked, tentatively, if that were for sale. She said it was, but there was no way to get it out for a test drive. Hmm. We turned our attention to the Cadillac. It turned out a tire was soft and the car was absent a battery. Stephen removed the battery from the owner's car, using his coke to loosen the connectors, and eventually got it into the Cadillac. He pumped up the tire. By that time his shirt was sopping wet and we were both red with bites. Stephen was feeling slightly resentful for having to share his coke with battery connectors. We climbed gamely in, however, and, with semi-high hopes, turned the ignition. When it fired right up, we looked at each other in triumphant surprise - until we realized our view was rapidly dimming in a huge cloud of white smoke! This was not just a little puff. Anyone driving by might have thought there was a forest fire. We naively hoped (or was it wishful thinking) that this was because the car had been parked for so long. We decided to drive it a few miles. The smoke followed us all the way. We drove carefully back, praying we wouldn't get ticketed for polluting the air. We quickly decided this was not The Car.

Desperate, we called the shifty-eyed owner of a Jimmy 4x4 we had seen parked on Main Street. It was clean and respectable looking, but we had been leery because the odometer was broken, and while the claim was 200,000 miles, who knows? Further, it was displayed at the home of a friend of the owner's. The owner himself lived in the next county. Perhaps the owner wanted to remain anonymous after the sale? Fortunately, it had been sold that morning. We had once again been saved by the Universe.

Yes, Stephen did finally get his car. That week the local paper came out with a new listing - a little Toyota. The owner had purchased it for his girlfriend and had worked on it long and hard. His honey then decided it was too small, and wanted something else. What can a guy do? We ran over to see it. We held our breath. It was actually as described (!!). It had a live battery. It had decent tires. It had a working motor. Nothing fancy, but after what we'd been through it looked like a dream. It was a stick shift, but after a couple of erratic and entertaining circuits of town, Stephen had his wheels. The search was over.

And what has this adventure to do with bridge (I know you are wondering)? I was reminded of our first search for a bridge partner. As we investigate, we find an assortment of characters. Some players poke along, like a worn-out old truck, and fall apart when the action gets too fast and furious. Some put up a good front, but can get really hot and fired up over any little thing (they evidently have a loose wire - or two). Some are glamorous, the Cadillac type, but operate in a cloud of smoke, seemingly oblivious to everything around them (except the mirror). Still others have played so long (200,000+ miles and climbing) their ability to change has come to a stop - their odometer is broken. We are lucky when we finally find a good steady player, like a little Toyota. Nothing fancy perhaps, but reliable and dependable. We may make a few false "jumps and starts" getting to know each other, but in the end we ride smoothly off and know we'll get there.

At long last we've found a winner.

"...May you find what you're seeking wherever you roam." - Irish Blessing.

* * *

THE TRUST FACTOR

"Our distrust is very expensive." – *Ralph Waldo Emerson.*

Bridge is a partnership game - we hear this often. Just what does "partnership" imply?

A solid partnership blends cooperation, hard work, and continuous communication. You collaborate with your partner. You set goals; you decide how to reach those goals. Your convention card is discussed, re-discussed, and sometimes just plain cussed. You decide what conventions to use, how to use them, and what your style will be. Most importantly –

YOU FOLLOW YOUR OWN RULES UNTIL YOU MUTUALLY DECIDE TO CHANGE THEM. That is TRUST.

This is especially important at the beginning of a partnership, when both partners are getting used to each other.

I am reminded of a new partner I played with years ago. At first he made wild and "innovative" bids and plays. I kept up my steady pace, played by the rules, and said nothing. Quite hard for a woman. After a few sessions, my partner played much better bridge. He trusted me; I had my bids, and I had my passes. We then did consistently well - it was worth the struggle. My tongue was sore for a while, though.

When you have a partnership in progress, and have laid out the basics, keep a notebook on your agreements. Once they're in writing there can be no disputes! Then bid and defend as agreed. Keep notes on the success or failure of new conventions. If something isn't working, change it – and *write it in your notebook*. Communication (both written and verbal) boosts trust like nothing else can.

If you are unsure of what might be out there that would make your game better, take some lessons together, or share a book on a topic of your choice. If this results in a change in your system - guess what - *write it down*. In this way you can keep your Trust Factor alive.

It is healthy to read your notebook over once a week or so, at least in the beginning, and more frequently after a change is made. Mistakes are common early on, as one would expect, but the fewer the better, and memory enhancement through a bit of study will turn you into a genius in your partner's eyes. Soon you will be sailing along, each knowing your system, trusting each other with your lives - or at least with your masterpoints.

Trust is also vitally important when one person is mentoring another, helping him climb the bridge ladder. It gives a partnership stability and security.

I've seen many a beginner wearing that well-known confused look. His partner, trying to make up for the beginner's inexperience, has overbid, underbid, or taken a flier into outer space. The beginner wonders what he missed. This does not sound like what he was told earlier were the "rules".

Both teacher and beginner can relax if the more experienced player simply follows the road map. The mentor resolves to submerge his own ego for the good of the partnership. Taking a few bad boards often makes an impression which weeks of lessons will not.

I must confess, I have learned the hard way myself. Partner and I had just agreed to play weak jump shifts in competition. I opened 1-H, my LHO bid 2-C, and partner bid 3-D.

There were stars in my eyes. I drove all the way to 6-D with my oh-so-appealing two-suiter. After being doubled, vulnerable, and going down 1100, I realized all was not as I had envisioned. I never forgot the competitive WJS again. My tactful partner remained silent throughout.

If a mentor makes a creative deviation from the expected bid or play, the logic involved is subsequently explained. If a beginner makes a mistake, the preferred bid or play is outlined later, and he begins to see the light. He maintains his trust in his partner and his skills become well honed. There are no bewildering pyrotechnics (like screaming, "You dunce!") to unnerve him. Hard going initially, perhaps, but the end result is gratifying. You both had a vision, and worked hard. Now you both can enjoy the results, as you rack up those points.

So, to engender success, be a trustworthy and supportive partner, and mentor. You will win more often, and more importantly, will preserve a smooth-flowing relationship.

You might even find this to be effective in "real" life.

"I'm not upset that you lied to me, I'm upset that from now on I can't believe you." – *Friedrich Nietzsche.*

" My teacher said I'd get better results if I trussed my partner! "

∗ ∗ ∗

HEARTBREAK HOTEL

"Well, since my baby left me,
I found a new place to dwell,
It's down at the end of Lonely Street
At Heartbreak Hotel." - Elvis.

I struggled along, took beginning
lessons, worked my way up, read, studied, tried
out a few partners. Finally, my efforts
appeared to pay off. A good player was
interested in starting a steady partnership. I
was elated. Wow! This was great. Just what
I'd been hoping for.

We coordinated our card, discussing every
nuance. We played together twice a week, and
began to see good results. I felt like a real
part of the bridge scene at last. I was
becoming *established*.

One overcast day, my partner called out
of the blue. "Hey, Suzy, I'm sorry to call at
the last minute, but I've been asked to play
with a newcomer to help her get acquainted, and
I just knew you'd agree this is what we all
should do. Do you mind if we cancel today?
We'll get together next week, OK?" Well, what
could I say? "Uh, sure, no problem. Later,
then, Boots." This was a surprise. But then,
we do have an obligation to welcome new players
into the club. It was too late to get another
partner, so I decided to finish mopping the
floor. Exciting.

A few days later, Boots calls and, again
apologizing, says she feels she must continue
with her mission for the poor newbie, since
Missy hasn't really met anyone else yet who is
up to her level. Hmmm. At least she called
early enough this time that I could get another
partner. Nice of her.

A few days later, I arrive at the club to play, and there they are, heads together, apparently quite intent on discussing their game. Boots looks up, gives a quick "Hi," and immediately gets back to her prior conversation. I feel a bit miffed. She has barely acknowledged my presence. Wow.

Of course, you guessed it, another call comes. It may take another week or so, Boots tells me, before she can feel right about leaving poor Missy. Well, okay. I line up partners in the meantime.

A Sectional is coming up, so I call Boots to make arrangements. Surely by now Missy has found a partner she wants to try out. Boots is a bit hesitant. Finally, she confesses. "Well, I'm so sorry, Suzy. I feel more in sync with Missy than I realized. I'd really like to play with her full-time. Naturally, you and I could still play together once in a while. I've learned so much playing with you and I'm forever in your debt." Blood drains from my face, I feel my heart racing, I don't know what to say. I certainly don't feel I can say what I would *like* to say. So I don't say anything. I just gently put down the phone.

How did this happen? Did I do something wrong? How could Boots be so cruel? What a blow.

I decide not to play that day. Instead I have a leisurely lunch, accompanied by a glass of wine, or two, or three. Then I call my good friend, Katy.

I cry into the phone, telling it all. Katy soothes me. She explains that Boots is always like this, jumping from partner to partner, thoughtlessly leaving a trail of bewildered partners behind. She assures me it is *not* personal. I am somewhat mollified, and instead of doubt, I begin to feel rage. How dare she? What a backstabber. I cannot believe I fell for her line. What a fool.

I ask Katy to play, and she agrees. When I enter the playing room, I feel all eyes are upon me, wondering why I'm not playing with Boots. I hope Boots isn't there. The doubts begin all over again. However, Katy joins me quickly and steers me over to the hospitality table. We talk and laugh and carry on like nothing in the world could possibly be wrong. I begin to feel much better. When Boots comes in I pretend I don't even see her. As we play, nobody mentions a thing, or asks about why Boots and I are not partners today. I begin to realize everyone probably knows Boots better than I do.

Time passes, and I get another steady partner. She and I get along well and we agree to be up front with each other from the get-go. I don't worry, just go with the flow. I now realize that, sooner or later, all things change; it is a natural progression in life. We have what we need now, and later we will have what we need later. I trust in Providence.

As Elvis croons, "You make me so lonely baby, I get so lonely, I get so lonely I could die." But I didn't die, and I won't. A new partner, and a few wins, will be my best revenge.

* * *

SHOULD I PLAY WITH MY SPOUSE?

"There is no peace among equals because equality doesn't exist in this universe. Either one prevails and the other follows, or both negotiate their differences and create a greater partnership." – Harold J. Duarte-Bernhardt.

This is an age-old question.

First of all let me say that I am not against playing with your spouse. I am just against playing with *my* spouse...

There are many factors that enter into this equation. You may feel you owe it to your spouse to ask if he or she wants to learn bridge and play with you. Do not feel obligated. Sometimes it is best to let sleeping dogs lie. It may be judicious to let certain opportunities for togetherness pass you by in the interests of the "till death do us part" kind of togetherness.

Married couples tend, after a while, to take each other for granted. They feel they can say just about anything to each other and be understood. They also expect a lot of each other, and want to be able to rely on their mate's intelligence and protection. A spouse may not realize that the bridge arena does not equate to the privacy of one's living room. It is a competitive, ego-filled battleground, full of uncertainty and pitfalls. It takes a lot of self-confidence and flexibility to escape unscathed. New environments can be unsettling. A spouse may appear, at the bridge table, to resemble Frankenstein. "Who is this person?" his mate may wonder. Love does not always conquer all. It needs a lot of help.

In fact, a story is told about a woman who shot her husband when he trumped her Ace – for the third time. She was acquitted. The foreman was said to be a bridge player.

A great deal depends on temperament and personality. Is your spouse an outdoors person? Is he always on the move, doing, going, never sitting still? I doubt that he would like sitting in a room full of characters for 3+ hours trying to learn a foreign language, all for some kind of ephemeral "master points".

On the other hand if your spouse loves games, puzzles, meeting a variety of personalities, he might enjoy your favorite hobby. If your spouse is also analytical and competitive he would probably fit right in.

Has your spouse ASKED about joining you in your hobby? This is a major key. If you have played for a while, are really getting into it, and your spouse still hasn't made a move or shown interest, it probably won't happen. This is a clue not to ask him/her to join you. Your ever faithful and loyal partner may feel they should say "yes" just to please you. Wrong answer.

Another key is how far your spouse would have to go to catch up with you in the bridge experience. It is generally easier for a partnership to begin learning and playing at the same time, so that they are at somewhat the same level. This way there is no temptation for the more experienced spouse to play the expert, to continually advise, teach, admonish, and even, heaven forbid, criticize - sometimes even in a loud voice with extreme facial expressions (not that I know anyone like this).

It can be an especially delicate situation when the wife is the more experienced player, and the marriage is fairly traditional. The questions of decision making, power, and gender roles can come into play. A husband may not be used to taking lessons from his wife, or having suggestions for improvement made by her. (My poor husband is quite used to that type of treatment, I'm afraid. And he doesn't even play bridge.) This can initially cause friction and a feeling of insecurity on the part of the beginning bridge player/husband. He may even feel threatened. The wife must be prepared to use the utmost tact and diplomacy, and prepare a lot of candlelight dinners. The upside is that the experience may broaden both persons' views and habits and actually enhance the relationship in the long run. If you are not both having fun within a few months, however, you may want to redesign your goals. Sometimes bit-sized pieces of time away from glaring lights are the way to go, rather than long drawn-out tournaments.

Of course if the desire and innate ability is there, a spouse can be a fun partner. Once you get the basics down, you are usually in sync, since you understand each other well, which boosts your potential for success considerably. The trick is that at least one of you should have a very loving, go-with-the-flow, forgiving nature. The type that doesn't hold grudges. The type for whom the experience is worth all else. Keep this in mind.

If you are playing with your spouse, it is also a good idea to periodically take time out from bridge to go for a quiet romantic interlude. This helps recharge and prioritize your relationship. Do not take any cards.

If you are a more experienced player, have read all the above, and still want to play with your spouse, then you must give yourself some strict guidelines (unless of course this is your way of getting a divorce without even trying). Remember, frustration is not born of reason. It is ego, it is wishful thinking, it is influenced by the desire to win. It is a natural, but not helpful, human emotion. It can be avoided by training yourself to use a positive approach. Each experience can be seen as an opportunity to iron out wrinkles and fine-tune your system. If partner doesn't have your expertise it can be a good time for a quick lesson from a gentle teacher. Harsh glares and rough words only increase poor partner's nervousness and that can crowd out all benefit, not only during, but after the game.

As you can see, self-discipline and self-control are prime when playing with a spouse, a friend, a pick-up partner, anyone. They are also great tools in "real life".

Of course one answer to this dilemma, a sort of have your cake and eat it too solution, is to encourage your spouse to take lessons and find a regular partner of his own. This way you can go to your local club together, travel to tournaments together, yet avoid the stress of competing together. You can compare notes afterward, revel in your individual glories and blame the rest on your respective, non-spouse partners.

Do I play with my spouse? Not at the bridge table. We are definitely not a 24/7 kind of couple. We enjoy our together-time – dining out, cruising, family vacations at the beach. We also enjoy the space our respective hobbies give us. I'm a bridge addict, he is a Las Vegas trekkie. By the way, in case you are skeptical at this point, we have been married 33 years.

I have a regular bridge partner, however, and believe me, it can be hard enough playing with your best friend, never mind your spouse. Sometimes I think the only reason my partner and I have survived over 20+ years of bridge is that we don't have to go home together. We are both first-borns and both Taurus's. Need I say more? However, we are also good communicators and very persistent. We are both total bridge nuts. We have similar interests outside of bridge (yes, sometimes there is life outside of bridge). So we have survived and enjoyed the journey.

I did run across a rare couple who has been married for 45 years and has spent 35 of those years playing bridge together. They assure me they still speak to each other - on Sunday mornings, around 8 a.m. Even they are not immune, however. They confess they do say things to each other they wouldn't dare say to other bridge partners, but they always manage to return to the bridge table the next day in good spirits.

Back to "Should I play with my spouse?" Only *you* can answer that one. Think it over carefully. Remember, you will not only be bridge partners, you will bring your marriage with you. Then, whatever your choice, go out, bring home those masterpoints, and have a great time.

PS - I wouldn't recommend keeping a loaded gun in the house…

"All married couples should learn the art of battle as they should learn the art of making love." - Ann Landers.

***

DIE-REC-TORRR!!

"I made a game effort to argue but two things were against me: the umpires [director] and the rules." – Leo Durocher.

A Beginner's Birds-Eye View

The Call
Oh, no, not again. The opponents have made that dreaded "Director" call. The worst of it is, I don't know what I've done – but I can't admit it! Then they'll know I'm a *real* beginner. I do know I haven't led out of turn, or reneged – especially since we haven't even started to play the hand. I'll just sit here looking guilty and hope for the best.

The Director arrives at the table with a questioning look, asking for the crime and the evidence. I smile sweetly. The opponents explain that I paused significantly before passing. *Paused*? Wow, thinking before you bid is not allowed?? I was just trying to remember if my partner's bid was one of those "conventions" we had talked about – that's all. I finally gave up, deciding I would never come to a conclusion, and took the coward's way out. I passed.

The Director looked at my hand, looked at my partner's hand, appeared puzzled, said we had our bids and to call him again if there was a question of any damage. Damage? My brain was damaged, that's what. Whew.

The Reason
I learned later that an experienced player can deduce information about his partner's hand when his partner makes an exceptionally long pause. The pause makes it clear partner has a problem and does not know what to do. Cards (points) can be placed in partner's hand. For example, one player opens,

there is an overcall, and responder then stares
into space for 10 minutes. Now opener knows
partner has some points, does not have a fit,
and is looking for inspiration. Legally,
opener cannot take advantage of that pause, or
bid in any way that he would not have bid had
there been no pause. Opponents protect
themselves from subsequent illegal action by
calling the director immediately. First, the
pause is established. The director then
instructs everyone on how to follow up.

This game is complicated.

Resolution
Having discovered director calls aren't
personal, I no longer feel guilty. I know the
director takes everything into account and
balances the scales when necessary. Meanwhile
I am learning what and what not to do. It's
part of the process. Bridge players want to be
sure they get what's coming to them, and more
if possible. I can even envision myself
calling the director someday...

Now I almost feel sorry for directors.
They put themselves on the line daily. They
listen to players bicker and throw tantrums and
cite all sorts and kinds of offenses. They
have to apply the judgment of Solomon. It's
not my idea of fun. I applaud their strong
constitutions. Without them our game would be
in a shambles.

The Directors
Directors don't just appear out of
nowhere. They have to take an extensive exam
through the ACBL. They have to be conversant
with ACBL laws, duplicate decisions, computer
software, and the Rules and Regulations. They
pay for this privilege.

It's more than rules, too. A good
director has to run bridge games of all types.

28

He needs public relation skills to balance his role as referee, judge, teacher, psychologist and entertainer. A sense of humor is paramount. So is a thick skin.

A director must be quick on his feet. He cannot ponder for hours over a ruling. He must know where to find information and find it fast. He must make his decision firmly and fairly, and if challenged, know how to proceed. A committee can be arranged to review a questioned decision, but meanwhile the game must go on.

The director has personal challenges - he must not show favoritism toward a friend, a benefactor of the club, or an expert. I remember an embarrassing moment in our local club. Willy was a good man, volunteered a lot of time and wine, and supported the Unit generously. However, he was known to be a bit temperamental. In this instance, he became *quite* frustrated with his partner, let out a curse, slammed down his cards, and walked out. This is *not* done. One's partner is embarrassed and alone; the other players have to cope with a ruined movement; and the director hyperventilates. I wondered what would happen next. Despite Willy's valued presence in the Unit, the director suspended him from the game for 3 months. A hard penalty, but I was gratified to see a precedent set, requiring good behavior by one and all.

Stories
        Directors always have stories. One director reminisced about his early years when he constantly listened to other directors give rulings. The ruling itself and the way it was given provided helpful tips. He had a mentor to whom the newbie brought problems for suggested solutions and discussion. If you want to direct, these are good practice tools. The ACBL Bridge Bulletin includes a *Ruling the*

Game column which covers unique problem calls and situations. It is instructional for directors and players alike.

Some directors have to be magicians. A frantic call brought a director to a worried-looking group who confessed a hand was missing. They had looked everywhere. He calmly reached to the back of a bidding box and pulled out the missing cards.

One dark and stormy night, a sweet senior, and new player, was declarer at 3NT. The opening lead was the Queen of Diamonds. Dummy's diamond holding was A8765. Declarer asked about the opponent's lead agreements, since the lead looked strange to her. Her RHO advised the lead of a Queen against a NT contract "absolutely, positively requires the Jack be played." Declarer called the director. When he arrived, declarer asked if the explanation could possibly be true. She was told that it was allowable and comes up frequently. Declarer muttered "Ok, but I don't like that." She called for the 5 from dummy. The director was ready to walk away when he noticed after RHO played the 2, declarer played the Jack! She announced, "I think this ruling is very unfair and I am going to quit playing here." It was then the director realized the confusion created by the wording of the explanation. The novice declarer thought *anyone* who held the Jack had to play it. Oops. As it turned out, declarer made 3NT for a top board. The only way the contract could be made was to drop the Jack on the first round. The Rueful Rabbit would have been ecstatic. The poor director wanted to explain everything but had to leave the room temporarily to control an oncoming fit of laughter. The woman was somewhat mollified by her top, but still thought this club was mighty strange.

Ethical Problems
     Directors have difficult personal
decisions to make. They want to play, but need
to direct as well. Is this legal? The ACBL
does not bar this. The number of masterpoints
awarded is not reduced when a director plays.
In a small club this usually presents few
problems. Everyone works together and sorts
things out.

     What happens when a director personally
pre-makes the hands? Many feel the director
and his partner should not, under these
circumstances, be eligible to win masterpoints.
However, the ACBL does not prohibit this
practice. Directors who own a club have the
right to play and to earn points. If a player
disagrees with this policy he can explain his
position to the director. If not satisfied, he
can play elsewhere, or perhaps donate a
mechanical dealing machine to the club.

Going With the Flow
     We will all have the dreaded "Director"
call made on us. Sometimes we will be guilty,
sometimes not. We want equity restored to us
when opponents make an error or breach the
rules, so we always welcome the director's
arrival. We make his job easier by pleasantly
relaying the details when asked. We thank him
as he leaves - and mutter under our breath
afterward.

What about you?
     A director is crucial in maintaining
harmony and order. Good directors are always
in demand. Perhaps you would like to direct?
You would be in the thick of things. You would
build your knowledge of the game. You would
have adventures. You would earn a few dollars
on the side as well.

     For some, directing is their passion and
profession. These men and women are a special

breed. We often take them for granted, these tireless protectors of the innocent. They travel from tournament to tournament, work long and hard, and often get little thanks. They enjoy keeping the peace, however, and feel, rightly so, that theirs is an important job.

We know it is, and are thankful for their presence.

"You cannot assault a referee [director]. He stands between the game and chaos." -Tony Banks.

* * *

EXTENDED FAMILY

"Every human being has hundreds of separate people living under his skin." - Mel Brooks.

Bridge is a captivating game, always evolving, never boring. We meet unique and distinctive characters who stretch our parameters. We belong to an international organization, a *really* big club, and are able to play against the best talent in our field. Bridge clubs are everywhere, so there's no withdrawal when we travel.

We play for all these reasons. For me, there's another reason as well. I am basically an introvert and am in the minority in the general population. In the bridge world, however, or so it is reported, the majority of the players are introverts. Bridge supplies me with needed social contact, makes me feel I belong to a special group, and gets me out of myself. The people in my bridge club and bridge world are part of my extended family.

We are often urged to be kind to our partners, which is good advice. However, we sometimes forget to be nice to our "extended family." It is gratifying to come to a table where the opponents greet me, smile, ask how I'm doing. It brings me into the whole picture. I remember one couple who were always quiet and aloof. I didn't know them except to play against and had no clue of what they were like. One day I noticed the woman always wore earrings which perfectly matched her outfits. I commented on this and expressed my admiration. She gave a big grin, started talking, and turned out to be a delightful, well-traveled individual who had many fascinating tales to tell. All this from a pair of earrings.

One elderly man, retired, always had an elf-like twinkle in his eye, but seldom spoke. One night at our club Christmas party this man rose to give out awards. He sprang to life. His charm, wit and humor kept us all enthralled and amused. I had missed out on months of his company because I was too reticent to make the first move, to interact with one of our own.

Of course there is a practical reason for all this niceness as well. Your opponent today might end up being your partner tomorrow. You could discover a beginning player who has talent and just needs a boost. You may be a beginner who finds a mentor. We all have something to give each other, even if it's only a word of encouragement, a recipe, or advice on how to install windshield wipers.

Let's take a look at some of the characters in our extended family who enrich and enliven our lives.

The Guardian

The Major walks briskly in (I curb an impulse to salute). A semi-frown accompanies his roving eyes as he searches the club for any sign of disorder. He finds all is well; he can relax - for now. He gives a painful half-smile and nods, his eyes still wandering. Once play starts, the Major is in his element. The director hovers close by. A nervous opponent looks at her cards, looks at the bidding box, looks again at her cards, and - passes. "DIRECTOR!" is heard all across the room. The Major sternly assures his opponent, "Nothing personal, you know. Good ethics, very important, must learn, ahemm." You can imagine him chewing on a cigar in bygone days. A collective sigh seems to pass through the room. "At least there are only two boards per round tonight," is whispered at a far table. What few know, however, is that in the backrooms of the District, our club is well known for its scrupulously ethical players – all having been educated by The Major. Meanwhile, long-term club members clue newcomers in about our special sergeant-at-arms well in advance. The new members feel welcomed, part of the in-crowd, and somewhat reassured.

The Player
Ava approaches our table, serious, focused, all business. She and her partner are seemingly invincible, constantly taking lots of points from the rest of us. She greets us with a thin smile. We play, and I make an error on defense. "Why Cathy, that is just not like you," she laments. "Did you have a late night? That switch was *so* obvious." I shrug, with a philosophical smile. Not quite what I feel like doing... I realize that she views me as her bridge peer, and that her sense of humor leans toward the dark side, so I give her some slack. Later, I find out her husband died at 52, her only child lives in London, and she doesn't work. She pours all her energy, which is considerable, into bridge. I decide to be nice. I compliment her. I know she loves classical music, and ask if she has any new CDs to recommend. She becomes another person. She now tells me how much she admires my articles in our Unit newsletter, and how she wishes she could be that creative. She looks sadly envious. My partner and I occasionally play on a team with Ava and her partner. It all works.

Hollywood
I look up. Roz, red hair flaming, ample assets swinging and bouncing, is descending upon us. Her three inch heels do not impede her one ounce. You would never believe she is 60. Here goes my concentration. I love this woman but oh my goodness. She greets me instantly, "Hi, Baby Doll, how ARE you? I just know you've got more news about your project."

Well, uh …

"I've been busy too, and you just wouldn't believe, it's too much, and when my ex - Oh, it's my bid?" Roz is our club's glamour queen, dressed to the nines, day or night, matching jewelry, perfect makeup. She's always in the thick of things. Every tournament, there she is, lined up with Marge, Joe, Kitty, Pat, she loves them all. And they all adore her. Before retirement she designed shoes; the stars were her biggest fans. She has a lifetime of energy and never stops. Even as she perpetuates her ditzy image, she is planning her next move. And talking. Yet never a negative comment escapes her lips. You may seldom get a word in edgewise, but you're by no means bored. Her stories are endless.

Lost Soul

Scott jerks over to the table, almost tripping over his own feet. He takes a seat and tucks his long legs under the chair. He gazes in my general direction, says hello, and tries to smile. He stoops over the cards in concentration. He yearns to be part of the group, but doesn't quite know how to go about it. He does his share, and gladly, but is just plain awkward. He's not too shy, however, to help his partners improve. In his best instructional manner he remonstrates, "Joe, did you forget we were playing DON'T, (frown), you can't miss these things, we'll never win."

One day Scott was approached by an old buddy, now a desperate tournament coordinator. His hospitality volunteer had abandoned him by inconsiderately moving to California. Scott resisted, but his sense of duty did him in. He finally agreed to tackle the job. To his amazement, club members went to Pango Pango and back to aid and assist. They cheered him on, propped him up, and, most importantly, provided lots of food. Scott forgot to be defensive and shy. The light came on. His contribution, his effort as one of the group, was needed, was appreciated. He now walks with a confident and more relaxed air. "I really am part of this community," he reflects.

The Volunteer
        "Here's a signup list for hospitality for our next tournament. You can bring your specialty morning, noon, or night. Any day is fine." You duly bring your contribution into the hospitality room at the appointed time. "Just put that dish right here, don't worry, I'll take care of it, you're just great, thanks. That's exactly what we needed." You feel exalted.

        That's our Trudy. A professional volunteer, big smile, bustling around with purpose and energy. We must have her. She's been all over the world, and found a way to volunteer every time. She must be 50, but still wears spiked blonde hair, a mini-skirt and clogs. She will never age, and never wear out. She could give lessons to the Energizer Bunny. Her spirit is to give. Ours is to appreciate. We do have to watch out for her at the bridge table, however. She is sharp and cutting, no holds barred. Wins a LOT. These volunteers aren't all motherly fluff.

A Gift From India
        Swapen, with his jaunty strut, bursts into the room; it is immediately brighter. There is a huge open smile on his face, and your name on his lips, no matter who you are. He knows more people, and more names, than I do after 20 years. It is absolutely embarrassing. Competition is his food and drink, but it is never personal. He thrives on bridge like a beaver building his dam. Day or night, when not out of the country researching for his University, he is at the bridge table. His child-like fervor is infectious. It reminds me of my early bridge years when everything was

shiny bright new. There comes a day when he
moves away. His attitude of wonder and delight
go with him. Nothing has been quite the same
since.

Perfection Itself
Mary is friendly, helpful, tried and
true. She volunteers. She smiles. She never
barks at her partner. She mentors beginners.
Worst of all, she is a good bridge player. Do
you know anyone like this? Neither do I. I'm
glad, because I'm sure I wouldn't like her.
But my partner sure wishes she knew someone
like this...

Directors
Directors can be quite diverse
characters. They too have their own styles and
personalities.

Experts Beware
Frank is called to the table to
straighten out a little problem. A card played
earlier by a new player was declared a penalty
card by the opposing "experts" and the guilty
player was told to leave it on the table. Now
the guilty one was on lead. The experts decide
this is the time to call the director. Frank,
protector of the innocent, declares that this
card can be picked up and there will be no
penalty. He advises everyone they should call
the director immediately, not later, when there
is a potential problem. The experts sputter in
self-righteous indignation. "Well," says
Frank, "I am the director and it's only a
penalty card if I say it is. Now get on with
things." And they do.

No Nonsense
Robert looks over his domain with no-
nonsense eyes, back erect, tie in place, shoes
spit-polished to a shine that blinds. When you
call him, you'd better be ready. "Stop,"
admonishes Robert. "One at a time." Then, "Is

that true Mr. Blue?" He delivers his judgment and walks away. That is the end of it.

Friend to All
Duckie, shirt slightly tucked in, hair askew, bounces over with a smile and inquires, "How may I help you?" He directs the inquiry in a friendly, but firm manner. He brings everyone into the picture, one at a time. His ruling is not challenged, and each player somehow feels he has been vindicated regardless of who was right or wrong. We love him.

Zen Buddha
Hilda moves with stoic serenity. She is a woman of few words. She always carries a copy of the "Laws". Her voice is never raised, she responds to emotion with fact, and does not tarry. "If there is still a problem later, call me again," she advises the persistent. Players know that begging and pleading, exploding or crying, will not faze this director. "I'm sorry, those are the rules," ends it all. One simply sighs and carries on.

You will note that in all cases, these successful directors have one thing in common. They carry an air of authority as their benchmark. They are firm and orderly. They know their stuff, and everyone is glad of it.

It's Our World
What variety, what a universal garden of human nature. I am so thankful for my extended family and appreciate each and every member. I know you do too. They help us get the most out of life - and more out of bridge.

"The bond that unites your true family is not one of blood, but of respect and joy in each other's life." - Richard Bach.

* * *

"It would be so nice if something made sense for a change." - Alice (Alice in Wonderland).

THE LOVE BOAT - WILL IT FLOAT?

Spring is in the air. I feel one with the heady flow of life as I walk into the club. I approach the partnership desk with optimism, and am rewarded with a smiling player of good physique, strong jaw, dark blue eyes, and a mass of dark wavy hair. I won't mind sitting across from him for three hours, I tell myself.

After one round, I am not so elated. My partner is quite charming, but seems to be researching the role of bridge expert for a movie. He will not win an Oscar.

After the game, Mr. Almost-too-good-to-be-true asks if I am single. I admit that I am indeed on my own. He then suggests that we take a short ride on his boat this coming weekend. The weather should be perfect, he assures me. His neighbors will be going too. I groan inwardly. He has all the qualifications for a first date, but really - his bridge is sooo bad. Could I stand it? Would I feel obligated to play with him if we went out? We certainly couldn't discuss any aspect of bridge without my getting heartburn. I decide to stall, and say that I am sorry, but my weekend is already arranged. He asks about a game tomorrow. Damn, this guy is persistent. I make another excuse, and he says he'll call me later then. He knows my number? Oh yes, it's in the Club Directory. Damn again.

I contemplate my seemingly strange priorities. The guy seemed nice. He got me coffee, laughed at everyone's jokes, admired our senior member's rock of a ring, went gaga over my endplay. He even mentioned that he was stopping by his mother's for a chat on his way

home. But bridge is half of my life. I know
other things should matter too. If he just
didn't play bridge it would be perfect. Should
I recommend bridge lessons? But he might want
me to give them to him, and that would be a
major migraine.

I decide to check with a few of my
friends who had chanced romance with fellow
bridge players. How had they balanced things
out?

First of all, they warned, check around.
Not every guy with a ringless finger is single.
Even the bridge world is not free of
opportunists, apparently. Surprise, surprise.
After that inauspicious advice, they told their
stories.

Malinda relayed how she had become quite
smitten with a Brad Pitt look-alike who played
excellent bridge. At the time she was a
relative beginner. She was excited to think
that she would be able to play up, and learn
from one of the best. She got more than she
bargained for from those bridge lessons. Her
partner was exacting and temperamental at the
table, and she was constantly tense and upset.
A friend asked her why she put up with it.
"He's such a good player," she moaned, her eyes
moist. When not at the bridge table, they
seemed to get along fine, but after a while,
the bridge persona of Mr. Wonderful came
between them. Malinda went her way, and
eventually married a quite promising player who
was also in the beginner's category. They have
a ball, at the table and away from it as well.

Bill and Lisa were both alone, their
respective spouses having passed on a year
before. Lisa just knew that Bill would love to
keep her company. After all, she was a great
player and a great cook. So she went after
him. He didn't resist too long.

Unfortunately, Lisa is quite competitive and assertive, and after the initial fluffy aura wore off, Bill became a bit miffed at all the scolding and carrying-on. Not one to let a good opportunity pass her by, Lisa determined to find a solution. She tells me now they play bridge only with other partners, so that when they leave together they can discuss rather than cuss.

Mac, case number three, said he knew from the get-go he didn't want to play, at the bridge table, with Clara. He had quite the thing for her, though, and told her so. He said he'd love to go out with her, but didn't want her to feel obligated to play bridge with him. He advised he had a steady partner and was committed to that arrangement. A tactful way to be up-front. They went out, were soon married, and have never once played bridge together. Smooth move, Mac.

June, on the other hand, tried the same tactic. It worked for a while, but then Greg got jealous whenever she would play with another guy. Fortunately, she found this weak spot before they got too entangled. They didn't stay a couple long.

After hearing all these confessions, I was still not sure what to do. I decided to wait and play it by ear. It wasn't long before Joe called and asked about boating that weekend. I said I would be free after a brief appointment with my hairdresser, and I would meet him at the dock, since it was close by. Were the neighbors still coming? "Oh, yes," he assured me, "they never miss a chance." I arrived, and was greeted with an enthusiastic smile. "And where are the neighbors," I inquire. "Are they on board already?" "Well, no," Joe admits, "they suddenly had other plans, but we'll have a great time just the two of us." I gave him a sharp look. "You know,

Joe," I reply, "I've just remembered I have other plans as well. Thanks anyway." I turned and walked away, thankful for that earlier appointment. Otherwise I wouldn't have my car. "And by the way," I turned to say, "my plans run through the winter." A bullet dodged. That's one decision taken out of my hands.

Who knows what I'll do next time. Love may be just around the corner, but which corner? I'll just have to keep my eyes and ears open, and take each case a step at a time. Meanwhile, I'll enjoy playing bridge with my extended family, and maybe volunteer for the hospitality suite. I might find somebody who wants to be hospitable.

. . .

A year later I ran into an old friend at the library and he wormed his way into my heart. He didn't play bridge, and still doesn't, and we both like it that way. We have other things in common.

"You are what I never knew I always wanted." - *from the movie,* Fools Rush In.

***

THE CLUB'S HUBS

*"Volunteers do not necessarily have the time;
they just have the heart." - Elizabeth Andrew.*

I wake with adrenalin pumping. This is
the Day. It's tournament time! "Breakfast?"
hubby inquires. "Sorry, honey, no time. Can
you catch a Hardees' biscuit?"

I fly out the door, pick up my partner,
and we swing by for our mandatory Starbucks
fix. Then it's on to fame and glory, we hope.
I calm down only when those thirteen cards are
in my hands.

At break, there's a fine spread. As we
chomp down, we review our successes and
disasters and head back into battle. When the
session ends, we invade the Hospitality Suite
for free goodies, and to absorb the gossip. We
eventually collapse, eagerly anticipating more
of the same for the next day.

I hate to admit, not once did we even
begin to envision the constant, frenetic,
behind-the scenes activity that a tournament
demands. Detailed planning is a must. Someone
has to budget for the tournament, arrange for
the site, and calculate the expected
attendance. Ample space must be insured, and
the tournament certainly can't run out of food.
Someone has to hire directors and caddies,
scrounge up volunteers for the partnership
desk, set up tables and chairs, put boards,
bidding boxes, and now, Bridge Mates, on the
tables. More someones have to entreat our
Unit's finest Southern gourmets to share their
delights with us, at the Hospitality Suite. Of
course it is mandatory to deliver a proper and
fitting bartender who can move quickly, think
on his feet, and entertain the crowd the whole
while. Finally, even more someones have to be

on hand to clean up the site each day. As you know, bridge players are notorious for their trashy ways; debris follows in their wake like the waves of a tsunami.

Just who are these many Someones? Volunteers.

These people are tireless. They love their "jobs" because they love bridge, and because they love the resultant camaraderie and beauty of a well-planned tournament. Volunteers are the hub of every club, of each Unit. Without these exceptional people, the wheels of bridge could not turn.

The stories volunteers have to tell make you laugh, cry, and sometimes gape in disbelief. They give great insight into our bridge community and human nature itself.

One particularly conscientious volunteer tells of working long and hard to provide a great hospitality room for her Club's Sectional. There were coffee and doughnuts, finger sandwiches, chips, veggies and dip, cakes, brownies, the works. There was a tablecloth and centerpiece. Still, some members were not happy that there was not a greater representation of "healthy" food, more veggies, some fruit. So, not to disappoint, our volunteer rushes out for grapes of every color, celery, carrot sticks, et al, for the next session. What does she hear then? Trish, you forgot the avocado! Trish took a deep breath, and suggested that the party in question become one of her volunteer team and run out for that avocado himself. The avocado lover made no further complaints.

One harried volunteer had to call her son in as an emergency volunteer. One of her crew had the flu; two employees of the pizza place which was to supply the between-session meal

decided to go to the beach. The young man
pressed into service ran to pick up the pizza.
He stacked his car high with hot fragrant
boxes. He perilously juggled his load into the
hotel – miraculously keeping every pizza
intact. He corralled some help, but still had
to make three trips himself. All this, and
he's not even a bridge player. Yet.

One tired volunteer took a short snooze.
The table was set, the session wasn't over for
an hour. A loud shout broke abruptly into her
fog, and she started awake. A large dog had
decided the cold cut tray looked much more
attractive than his usual dog food. It was
gone in an instant. The volunteer was in a
panic. The dog owner, red-faced and profusely
apologetic, promised immediate replenishment.
How and why the dog was there in the first
place never became quite clear.

Another circumstance created a new type
of volunteer. One avid player decided that
having a baby was no reason to drop bridge.
She started a tournament day-care center,
manned by volunteers. They had cribs, toys,
games, puzzles, even field trips for the older
kids. Food and supplies got expensive, so the
volunteers marketed toddler T-shirts sporting
the phrase "Bridge Kibitzer." What bridge-
playing grandparent could pass that opportunity
by? Once the Unit saw the benefits, and the
increased attendance, they voted to subsidize
the activity. Way to go.

An engaging couple in our Unit shares a
car. We all know the wife from her trips to
and from the center, carrying her bridge addict
husband back and forth. She quickly became an
honorary member of our bridge family. Once her
husband retired, she decided to take a more
active role in his hobby. No, she didn't learn
to play bridge. She was smarter than that.
She took on the role of volunteer. She is at

every tournament, a virtual whirlwind of activity, organizing, scurrying about, and assuring contributors that she absolutely couldn't do anything without them. Just goes to show, you don't have to play to be a valued member of the group.

If you would find it intriguing to work behind the scenes, to be part of the Inner Circle, to get to know Directors and other movers and shakers (even if only the salt shakers), think about being a volunteer. There are countless jobs that need attention. If you don't want to be directly involved in running a tournament or club game, there are always phone calls to make, e-mails to send out, snacks to bring. You can give lessons, learn to direct. The Unit newsletter can always use another article, or an editor. Announce your availability for the Board of Directors of your Unit. You will get an insider's view of what makes things work and keeps the game going. You will be part of an elite crew.

Now when I play I think about those of our group who make it possible for me to leisurely walk in, enjoy my favorite game, and go home without a care in the world. I thank them personally. I even volunteer my limited assets when possible. I feel more in touch with the whole process. Volunteers may do their jobs out of love, but they love to be thanked. So, thanks, to all of you.

"I can no other answer make, but, thanks, and thanks." - William Shakespeare.

***

BEGINNER NO MORE

"The journey of a thousand miles must begin with a single step." – Lao Tzu.

Your parents play bridge and bribe you to fill in from time to time. Friends at school twist your arm to provide a fourth. Cohorts at work coerce you into their noon game. You fall briefly in love with a duplicate player. Love runs its course, but you catch the bridge bug. You are hooked. You must have more.

You take lessons. You join the local bridge club. The 49er group feels just right.

You earn a few points and move to the 99er group. You are happy. You win a lot, have fun, feel comfortable. You know there's more out there, but for now you feel at home.

You begin to feel a bit bored. You take more lessons and start to play with a steady partner. You move up to the 199ers. You don't win as much but you make solid progress. This feels good. The big guys still scare you though. They talk about so many complicated conventions and coups. It sounds like a different language. You decide to stay put for a good long while.

In a few months, though, the language of the Open group doesn't sound so strange. You get bits and pieces here and there and it is intriguing. You wonder, "What would it be like?" Well,

JUMP RIGHT IN!

Get into the "big people's" pool. Be bold. Listen to your opponents when they talk about the hand, the opening lead, the conventions they use. Ask them questions. All bridge players love to give their opinions and show their knowledge. You will learn a bunch, and it's all for free.

Find a mentor, take more lessons, add a convention here and there to your card. Don't be afraid to experiment. Some new ventures will flunk big time, and others will give you great new tools for winning more often. You won't know which tools work for you until you try them out. Sometimes you need to ...

FALL OFF THE HORSE!

It's expected. It's part of the process.

Nothing burns a new convention into your brain like forgetting it and getting a big fat ZERO. Be thankful for that zero! I guarantee you, the next time that convention comes up you won't forget it. I learned promptly what a takeout double was after I doubled the opening bidder's 1H because I had AKJxxx of hearts. When my partner bid 6C I knew there was something rotten in Denmark – and it was me. I had fallen off the horse. But did I give up? No, no, no. I had to ...

GET RIGHT BACK ON!

My next partner (I never seemed to have the same partner twice in those days) could at least rely on my takeout doubles to really be for takeout. After all, I was back on the horse. I now had the confidence to ...

KEEP ON RIDING

After a few such escapades, you start to see the light. Your horizons expand. You read a book or two, find a steady partner, go to a Sectional, a Regional, even a National!

You have started a learning process which will last a lifetime. You are developing

56

friendships which will last a lifetime. You have begun an adventure which will last a lifetime. The lifetime guarantee is…

YOU WILL NEVER BE BORED AGAIN.

"You may be disappointed if you fail, but you are doomed if you don't try." – Beverly Sills.

* * *

GUT INSTINCT

"Intuition isn't the enemy, but the ally, of reason." - John Kord Lagemann.

Everyone writes about technique. You visualize the instructor standing at the podium, tapping his baton. "Attention, attention," he begins. Referring his class to the six-page chart on percentage plays, he admonishes, "You must have this vital information memorized inside out and backwards, or you will *never* be a good player." Wow. You wonder if it's worth it. After this comes the mere four-page chart on opening leads, followed by Chapters 7-11 on conventions everyone simply must must know.

Some players complain that once in a while they just like to fly by the seat of their pants. Do instinct and flair have their place?

The subconscious is a storehouse of information. It is constantly and silently putting together all that we see, think and do. It registers small sights and sounds that our conscious minds do not note as significant. It can communicate with us if we let it. It is always trying. When our minds are free of clutter, not blocked by doubt and fear, the subconscious can whisper in our ears. We often call this communication intuition, or label it creativity. No good player should be afraid to follow his "gut feelings."

I often hear a voice calling to me when I'm on opening lead. "Lead me, lead me," says the little 3 of Hearts. I look at my hand. I recall the bidding. I say, "What, are you crazy?" to that tiny voice. I then lead the nice big Q from a QJ9-D holding. Of course, dummy comes down with AK10-D. It turns out

that my partner has the heart KJ10 behind
dummy's Axx, and had I led from my Q53 we would
have gotten 2 heart tricks. Instead, they
disappear on subsequent sluffs by declarer.
Oh, well. So much for thinking things out
instead of following my instincts.

It's the same on defense. I know our
only hope is for my partner to have a certain
card, say the A-H, but the bidding says
otherwise. I am being urged by my gut to lead
a heart, but I chicken out. What a disaster if
pard doesn't have that card. Fear took a
chokehold. Of course, pard did have that card.
Why I chose to believe those tricky opponents
and their rotten bidding instead of my inner
voice is beyond me.

Here is an example from declarer's point
of view:

Through some optimistic but scientific
bidding, you and your partner reach 6H on these
hands:

> Ax
> K109
> KQJxx
> Xxx
>
> KQx
> AJxxx
> Axxx
> X

You open 1H, partner bids 2D, you raise
to 3D. Partner then bids 3S and you decide to
bid 4C, showing first or second round control.
Partner then bids 4H. Your hand is looking
better every minute, so you decide 6H is a good
gamble.

Your left hand opponent seems calm, no
frown creases her brow. She leads the A-C

without hesitation. This seems a bit strange, since you might have had the Kx of clubs for your 4C bid. But, after all, your side did bid each and every suit, and she had to lead something. Normally you would win the next trick and go to dummy with the K-H, finessing toward your hand against the Q-H. Those vibes from the opening leader are coming through good and strong, though. She seems just a bit too cool. Your gut feeling tells you she is sitting there with four hearts to the Q. You decide to back your intuition with action, and finesse toward the K109-H in dummy. Bingo. Making 6.

You were rewarded by having faith in your sixth sense.

So, if you believe the cards lie a certain way, whether by counting, inference or pure instinct, never fear to back your judgment. If a soft voice whispers seductively in your ear, listen to it. Creativity and intuition definitely have their place in bridge, as in real life. What fun would it be if everything were pure science? (I am *not* asking you engineers.)

"The intuitive mind is a sacred gift and the rational mind is a faithful servant. We have created a society that honors the servant and has forgotten the gift." – Albert Einstein.

* * *

SHADES OF GRAY
The Ethics Dilemma

"You cannot make yourself feel something you do not feel, but you can make yourself do right in spite of your feelings." - Pearl S. Buck.

Laws are delightfully plain and simple, black and white. They outline what you can and cannot do. They provide specific penalties for doing what you should not, or for not doing what you should. They do not, however, cover those gray areas, those fluid situations that can slip through the cracks.

"Oh," you say, "I know all about Active Ethics and Zero Tolerance. You have to be nice to everybody, and tell your opponents everything you know about your convention card when they ask." Well, that is true, and I am glad you know all that. Sometimes all that, however, is not all there is...

Struggling with the idea of ethics is usually far from our minds when we are in the heat of battle, competing for part-scores, moving toward slams, wishing those pesky opponents would just leave us alone. We can also feel the fire when defending a closely bid game that, if made, could lose us first place.

Duplicate bridge is an unusual game. It is competitive, yet we do not play for money. Many non-bridgers find this strange. "What *do* you play for?" they ask. I explain that we play for points, similar to chess ratings, which register our relative expertise in the bridge world. In other words, we play for glory. We also, of course, play for the love of the game. For most of us, that has to be enough. Those who are truly gifted and ambitious can go on to *earn* money playing bridge, as opposed to winning money. They market their skills by taking on clients, writing bridge books, teaching lessons.

Mainstream bridge players take full advantage of this pool of expert knowledge.

"Why can't you also play for money?" these curious friends ask next. I advise that bridge is considered a "gentleman's" game, and that we want to keep it as free as possible from the temptations that the glitter of money sometimes brings. We want to keep it ethical, above-board, and truly competitive for all players. Realistically, of course, we all know that the ego can be just as tempting a siren as money. The bridge world is constantly on the alert for those who feel they can ignore the Laws to get where they want to be.

This idea of a beautiful, complex, pure game, serving as a competitive field for players of all levels and abilities, is an ideal worth preserving. Ethics is considered by some the most important factor in our game. It is our silent partner, urging us to throw aside those ugly temptations and rise to the occasion. Ethics insures fairness, and encourage each of us to become our best bridge, and personal, selves.

"Okay, I'm convinced," you say. "But just what are all these temptations you are talking about? I'm not sure I would recognize them."

The guidelines are simple. You must not speak anything but the language of bridge. You must not listen to anything but the language of bridge. When you do otherwise, you are straying off the path.

"Well, isn't that what we all do?" you inquire. Hmmm. Let's look at some *other* languages.

Body Language

We have become a society well acquainted with body language. We use our knowledge of behaviorisms to understand what those around us are really thinking, are really telling us. It can be the same with bridge. The difference is that we ethically should not be speaking, or listening to, this language. How often do we see a worried glance, a rolling of eyes, eyebrows being raised, uncomfortable moving and shifting around in one's seat? You may hear an "Oh!" escaping from partner, as her hand flies to her mouth. These are telltale signals that something is wrong, a mistake has been made, a conventional explanation perhaps given incorrectly.

An ethical player must train himself to control his body language. An ethical player must steel himself not to take into account in any way the message sent by another's body language. Body language is not illegal. Sometimes we can't help being startled into giving ourselves away. If this is not a habit, it is certainly understandable. The vital follow-up to an inadvertent message of this kind is to *ignore* it. It is unethical to let it influence you in any way. You must bid, play, defend, as though you had seen or heard nothing. Not quite as easy as it appears at first glance.

One not so obvious example occurs in the bidding arena. You open; your LHO overcalls; your partner hesitates, reaches for the bidding box, pulls her hand away, reaches again, her hand hovering over the box indecisively. She finally pulls out the "Pass" card. Her body language has told you several things. She has some values; she doesn't have a raise of your suit; she doesn't know what to do. Having told you all this, she can now pass and leave it up to you. Right? You now know that this is NOT right. You must take any subsequent action based on your hand alone, assuming that partner had nothing to tell you.

Also included in body language is the fast pass or bid. This is especially significant after a preemptive bid by the opponents. It is thought by some that if a bidder did not pull out a "Stop" card, it is not necessary to hesitate 10 seconds. This is *not true*. After every preemptive or jump bid, an opponent is required to hesitate 10 seconds, or a reasonable facsimile thereof. If instead the opponent's hand whizzes to the Pass card and plunks it right down he might as well be saying, "Partner, be careful, I'm broke." On the other hand, if the opponent can't wait to get his 3H bid out of the box, he is exclaiming to the world, "Hey, look at me, I have a great hand and a great suit. I didn't even have to stop to think about this one."

When defending, we do sometimes have to pause to think. This is fine. Hesitating when you have no reason to do so, however, is unethical. This is especially heinous when declarer leads a card and you hesitate – with a singleton. Big no-no. The declarer might even call the Director when the hand is over if your unnecessary pause led him astray.

The English Language

We are often asked to explain our alerted bids. We know how to do this. We don't just say, "Puppet Stayman." We let the opponents know the particulars, that partner is asking if we have a 4 *or* 5 card major. We hope partner does not now let out a moan, evidence that she has forgotten our new agreement. Regardless, you will respond as your convention dictates, ignoring partner's evident pain.

There may be times when your partner is asked to explain a bid, and she makes an incomplete or incorrect explanation. You DO NOT use the English language to correct partner. You sit stoically, quietly, until the proper moment arrives. If your side becomes declarer, that is the time to correct your partner's misinformation. If you are defending, you must wait until the hand is over, so that you will not give partner information not due him, and then tell the opponents. They'll call the Director if they feel damaged.

The Language of Silence

How can keeping your mouth shut be unethical? There may be times that it's the smart thing to do, but unethical?

Sometimes we are sorely tempted. I must have warned Droopy Dave a million times to hold his cards up. I almost do it automatically before even looking his way. Every once in a while I think, what the heck, why not just take a peek and let him stew in his own juice. He's been told, hasn't learned his lesson, he deserves to be found out. I really want to be silent. But then I take a deep breath, keep my eyes averted, and one more time give Dave his faithful warning. To be silent would not be ethical. It would sure help me find that finesse, though.

When we forget to alert, or partner gives an incorrect explanation of an alert, we may be tempted to just keep quiet. After all, it may not make a difference. The opponents have barged into the auction and will just have to suffer for their impertinence. And how could they prove you knew anyway? You may have just forgotten. When the hand is over it may be that it didn't make a difference – to the result. But you were not only unethical, you violated a Law. Your reputation has begun its skid, and your soul is on its way to Bridge Hell. You hopefully end up so ashamed that you never keep silent again – at least not when you should be speaking up!

Psychic Bids
     Psychic bids are legal. It is illegal to
psych frequently, or to have specific
agreements, for instance, to psych only in
third seat after two passes. The psychic
bidder must be the only one who knows what his
bid means. So there is no problem with
psyching, right?

     Well, right. Ethically, however, there
is an exception. (There's always an
exception.) You are considered an insensitive
boorish cretin if you psych against novices.
Beginning players have enough problems without
having to contend with competitive bidding from
outer space that makes no sense to them
whatsoever. They become confused and
overwhelmed. They may feel like giving up,
like they'll never get this game under wraps
after all. We don't want that. We need new
players. We want to encourage and mentor them,
and so gladly give up some of our tricky ways
to bring them into the fold.

LET'S DO IT!
     How do we guarantee our own ethical
behavior? We must first be committed to
honoring our game and the members of our bridge
community. We must want to do the right thing,
and do it anyway even when we don't want to.
We must know our conventions inside out and
backwards, so there is never a mistaken
explanation, or a non-alert. We must speak
only bridge language, and listen only to bridge
language. If we do, by some twist or turn, get
unauthorized information from our partner, we
must bid and defend as if we see no evil, hear
no evil, speak no evil - and do no evil. Your
good reputation and behavior may even inspire
others to follow suit. It's the only way to
keep our great game truly great.

*"We have committed the Golden Rule to memory;
let us now commit it to life." - Edwin Markham.*

" Forget what I said about ethical behaviour
becoming the norm these days! "

* * *

YOU MEAN I HAVE TO BE NICE?
Zero Tolerance/Active Ethics

"Do all the good you can, by all the means you can, in all the ways you can, in all the places you can, at all the times you can, to all the people you can, as long as ever you can." – John Wesley.

Ol' Grizzle swept the room with an arrogant and impatient glance. He thundered up to the registration desk. "Give me Table #1," he barked, plunking down his dollar. "I've been gone awhile, but you can bet I'm still number one seed."

Little did Grizzle know that the entry fee was not the only thing that had been raised. So had the standards. Etiquette was in demand. Ethics were reinforced. By game time number one seed, scowling like a petulant child, sat sulking at Table 5. What a blow.

It took a while for some to become acclimated to the ACBL Code of Active Ethics, and Zero Tolerance Policy. Bridge had been a total free-for-all. It was common to hear yelling, name-calling, slamming of cards, banging of fists, loud angry "Director" calls. Partners freely berated and abused one another without penalty, shouting as opponents stared in stunned disbelief. If a session went by without incident, suspicious players would speculate, "Have the Russians dropped a 'nice virus' into our water?"

Directors could admonish and threaten, but had no concrete ACBL direction. The owner of a game would ban obnoxious players, only to have them take their undiminished pyrotechnics to the club down the street. Recycling at its worst.

The following true incident would scarcely have raised an eyebrow in the "bad old days." A man and wife were playing together. A violent argument erupted. Joe upbraided Madge for her bad bridge in general and, more specifically, for not bidding game on the last board. The opponents hurried them on to the next hand. Joe opened one heart. LHO passed. Madge sat perfectly still, arms folded, eyes flashing. She did not remove her cards from the board. "Four hearts," she snapped, glaring at Joe. All passed. Joe pulled out her cards, spread the dummy, and made his contract. He eyed Madge and remarked, "From now on, always leave your cards in the board. You do much better when you don't look at them."

Humorous, perhaps, but imagine having to put up with this kind of attitude and behavior time after time. In fact, a divorce attorney playing against the above pair handed them his card after one such round.

A flurry of complaints about negative behavior began to flood the ACBL. Members were incensed by players who attempted to gain advantage using questionable tactics. Unusual conventional agreements were not explained. Players would hesitate on defense with a singleton. New players were intimidated and driven away. Attendance was down at clubs and tournaments. ACBL membership overall was down. Something had to be done.

The Code of Active Ethics was formulated at the Fall, 1986 Atlanta NABC. The goal of this program was to insure fair and pleasant conditions at all levels of bridge. The message went out to all Districts, Units and Clubs that this was to be an *active* policy of education and reinforcement.

The "Alert" procedure sprang from the spirit of active ethics. It was put into effect on June 17, 1996. All unusual conventions, doubles, leads, et al, were to be announced with a spoken "Alert" or by using the

72

"Alert" bidding box card. This would provide equal knowledge and opportunity and bring fair competition closer to a reality. More commonly used conventions were merely to be "announced" aloud. For example, when a Jacoby transfer bid follows a NT opening or NT overcall, the term "transfer" would be spoken by the partner of the NT bidder.

The issue of antisocial and disruptive behavior was officially addressed when the Zero Tolerance Policy was formulated in the spring of 1998. The ACBL subsequently adopted Laws 74, 80F, 81C4, 90A, 91, and 92A. These laws outline policies (and penalties) in effect during NABCs and other ACBL sponsored events. Clubs, Units and Districts were strongly encouraged to adopt and enforce these laws.

A detailed summary of these innovations follows:

Code of Active Ethics
The philosophy of this Code is that winners should be determined solely by skill, flair and normal playing luck.

Principle of Full Disclosure: Information available to your partnership must be made available to your opponents. This includes information as to style. Is it your partnership style to make weak two bids on 5 card suits? With a four card major on the side? What quality is demanded of your suit? If an opponent inquires, this information must be given.

Social Behavior: An ethical player maintains a courteous attitude toward opponents and partner, and avoids behavior that would make anyone uncomfortable.

Slow Play: When a pair falls behind they must make up the time as quickly as possible. Slow play disrupts the normal progression of the game and distresses waiting players. Slow play is subject to penalty.

   Conventions: ACBL events list a chart of permitted conventions. Do not use a convention not on the chart. A pair must have a clear understanding of when and how to use conventions listed on their card. They must be able to appropriately inform opponents. Claiming ignorance is no longer an excuse!

   If you agree to play with a new partner and feel you will forget a convention he wants to use, it is best to say "No thanks," to start with.

Alert Procedure
   When your partner's bid has an unusual meaning, or is part of a convention marked in **red** on your convention card, you must say "**Alert**" and display or tap the Alert Card. When your partner's bid is one marked in **blue** on the convention card, you must **announce** its meaning verbally. If your partner's bid is marked in **black** on the convention card, **no action** is necessary. Stayman is one example.

   ACBL philosophy is that bridge is not a game of secret messages - the auction belongs to everyone at the table. Opponents are entitled to know the agreed meaning of all calls. When asked, the bidding side must give a full explanation of the agreement. Stating the common or popular name of the convention is not sufficient.

Zero Tolerance Policy
   The Mad Hatter is not allowed in Wonderland. Zero Tolerance sends bad boys back home to Mother (if she'll take them). The Golden Rule is the standard. Now new players feel welcome and the regulars can relax.

   Law 74A specifically prohibits:

1) Badgering, rudeness, insinuations, intimidation, profanity, threats or violence;
2) Negative comments concerning opponents' or partner's play or bidding
3) Constant and gratuitous lessons and analyses at the table;
4) Loud and disruptive arguing with a director's ruling.

Law 91A gives the director the authority to assess disciplinary penalties. A scoring penalty may be assigned, or, after repeated offenses, a player may be removed from the game, or suspended.

It is a regulation to have two clearly completed convention cards available to the opponents.

Poor Ol' Grizzle didn't last very long at the club. He just couldn't comprehend that he was no longer the center of the universe. Instead of being intimidated, the players merely looked at him as if he needed deodorant. He couldn't get partners. If he did pick up some poor unsuspecting soul, it was a one-day stand. I think he took up golf.

I must admit, I still have to bite my lip from time to time. I bring along Chap Stick just in case. I feel better for my self-discipline when the game is over, though, and so does my partner. We save all our discussions for after the game. When the heat of battle has passed, those minor boo-boos seem almost insignificant. Meanwhile our energy has been conserved and partnership rapport maintained. All thanks to Active Ethics and Zero Tolerance. Good going, ACBL.

"When I do good, I feel good, when I do bad, I feel bad..." - Abraham Lincoln.

PLAYING
AREA

***

THE INTIMIDATION FACTOR

"Obstacles are like wild animals. They are
cowards but they will bluff you if they can.
If they see you are afraid of them...they are
liable to spring upon you; but if you look them
squarely in the eye, they will slink out of
sight." - Orison Swett Marden.

What is it about certain players that
makes us quiver and quake? They intimidate us
just by being there. We do outlandish things
we would never otherwise consider. We can't
put a finger on it; we go into brain-dead mode
automatically.

This frequently happens when we encounter
a pair we know are experts, or at least
exceptionally good players. We psych ourselves
out. We prepare ourselves for a bottom. We
shoot ourselves in the foot before the round
begins. As Walt Kelly's Pogo once observed,
"We have met the enemy, and he is us!"

You know the scenario. You're having a
great game, you are up and alert, you know you
have a chance to win. You move for the
upcoming round and glance at the next table.
Oh my God, it's *them*. The bottom drops out of
your stomach. All your confidence evaporates.
You furtively whisper to your partner, "We
really have to tighten up here, don't let them
get one over on us." So you compete like crazy
and go down doubled in 4 clubs when their 3
spades doesn't make. Sound familiar?

Why do these players shake us up so?
Part of it, we hate to acknowledge, is our own
insecurity. If we were to continue our steady
game and treat the star opponents like anyone
else, we would have half a shot. In fact,
treating experts like anyone else can shake
them up. "Don't they know who we are?" they

ask themselves. Even the big boys are not completely immune to insecurity.

I remember well an incident when my partner and I proved this theorem. We were in the semi-final stage of a GNT (Grand National Teams) competition, Flight B. We were coming up against the pair who had won in our District the year before. They weren't experts, but somehow managed to push our buttons. One of the pair oozed self-confidence and had a superior smirk that seemed permanent. I took a deep breath and decided this was too important; I had to be strong. I walked right over with an oh-so-friendly smile and a casual "Hi, great to see you," as though I had not a care in the world. I have never seen them make so many mistakes. Our team prevailed and we went on to the next stage. And lost. But we were proud – we refused to be intimidated. Take care, however, lest you become an intimidator yourself. Once you get some wins under your belt, the temptation may arise. The line between intimidation and self-confidence can be mighty thin. Keep your golden reputation intact.

A few experts actually attempt to *enhance* the intimidation factor. They act pretentious and arrogant. They sit north/south so opponents have to come to *their* table. They raise an eyebrow when you make an unusual bid or play, as if your judgment is lacking, hoping to rattle you and sow seeds of doubt. They may call the director at every possible opportunity. They may bid and play outrageously fast as though, "There is nothing to this at all. What is the big deal?" They hope to confuse and unnerve you, and rob you of that moment you need to think. Alternatively, they may play or bid at an excruciatingly slow pace in hope you will fall asleep, or lose concentration (perhaps start thinking about dinner?). Such players are sure you will think

they are brilliant, instead of merely devious.
Personally, I feel they were never taught good
manners, or at least sloughed them off early in
their bridge life.

Ignore such behavior. Draw an invisible
space around you into which no negativity can
reach. Continue at your own pace. Be oblivious
to your opponents' tactics. However, if things
get out of hand and your opponents are
continuously outrageous, it will be your turn
to call the Director. He is there to insure
that *all* players are courteous and abide by the
rules.

Now I am not inferring that every expert
deliberately attempts to intimidate. Some
players intimidate by their very presence.
They can't help it. They are successful, their
position in the bridge world is secure, they
have an abundance of self-confidence. An aura
surrounds them and becomes part of their bridge
personality. We feel it and are in awe.

I am reminded of the late great Dave
Treadwell. He was charming, and a sit-down
comic - but his bridge was deadly. We were
playing against him and the bidding proceeded:

Partner	Opp. #1	Myself	Dave T.
1D	Pass	1H	Pass
2H	Pass	Pass	2S (without hesitation)
Pass	Pass	?	

I feel I should go to 3H with my 10
points, but am afraid we'll get doubled - after
all, these are experts! So I meekly pass. It
happens that Dave had balanced on a *three card
suit*. I was aghast. His partner had four
spades, and they made the bid, for a top. I
quickly added that tricky technique to my
arsenal.

As was Treadwell, the majority of experts are polite and generous. They answer questions; they give you a "well done" when you execute a tough play or find a creative bid. That's the kind of behavior we strive to emulate.

Some experts are also Pros. They have high stakes. They rely on their reputations to attract clients, who provide a large part of their income. They need to stay on top to sell their books and maintain their syndicated bridge columns. Some participate in bridge cruises. These perks all evaporate if their reputation starts to slide. If some experts are preoccupied or seem stressed you can understand why.

Away from the bridge table an expert is like the rest of us, with his own personal joys and sorrows. You come across an expert who is having a bad day and think, "What a grouch!" This person is usually outgoing and friendly, but it turns out his best friend died yesterday, or his wife left him, or he got a bottom playing against an opponent with only 50 masterpoints. He feels entitled to his mood; we might be a bit testy too if the tables were turned.

Meanwhile, create your own image. You are an integral part of the bridge world. Remember, experts started out as beginners, although they may not acknowledge this. A quiet, serious look makes opponents pause, but if this isn't your style, be your usual relaxed and friendly self. Get to know these opponents who seem to breathe in rarefied air. You may find experts are actually human.

Dress up a notch for a tournament. It gives you confidence and makes people take you seriously. Individuals who care about their appearance, it is thought, care about their bridge game.

Sit erect, look alert and positive. Which I'm sure you are. Double confidently and in tempo - take that red card out as though you had been waiting for just this opportunity.

Personally, I like to hire kibitzers. They hang on my every word and nod their heads as if in a trance. (Just kidding guys. Or am I?) And did I mention I'm off to visit my daughter at MIT after the tournament...

The real trick is NOT to be intimidated by intimidation. This takes practice and self-confidence. Don't look for tops every time, but rise to the occasion and do your best every time. If you play your usual thoughtful, brilliant game you can expect to come out at least average against a big pair - and once in a while you'll get that top you can brag about for the next six months. I still relay my story about coming up against Lynn Deas in a Regional pairs game and setting her 1100; of course I don't mention that it was ten years ago, or that she was playing with a client.

To quote Charles R. Swindoll, "Life is 10% what happens to you and 90% how you react to it." Resolve to drop your fear. Be bold. Approach an expert table with a calm, pleasant demeanor; act oblivious to your opponents' exalted aura. Greet the pair as you would any other. Give yourself an inner pep-talk. This is *your day*, and no one can take it from you. It takes practice, but you will prevail. And someday, you may be the expert everyone fears!

What a game ...

"If you know the enemy and know yourself you need not fear the results of a hundred battles." - Sun Tzu.

***

THE MIRROR

"A game is like a mirror that allows you to look at yourself." - Robert Kiyosaki.

Bridge is a microcosm of life.

Look into the magic mirror. Your strengths and weaknesses will be revealed, and a path toward transformation will materialize before your eyes. In other words - check out your bridge game.

Bridge is an integral part of you, your life, your social structure. It reveals clues about your approach to life, how you deal with others, how you react to stress. It provides a free tool for self-knowledge. It is your magic mirror.

It is a lot cheaper than therapy - well, a bit cheaper than therapy...

As images are revealed, rest assured, there is no good, better, best. Each individual approach to the game has special merits. The goal is to see yourself clearly, to find out what makes you tick. For example, you may wonder why you are constantly stymied by the play of the hand. An introspective inquiry into your psyche might help rid you of this mental block. It could give you insights that improve your game, and perhaps your "real" life as well.

PARTNERSHIPS
The Experience Factor
Do you like to play with a partner who is less experienced than yourself, more experienced than yourself, or on a par with you?

If you prefer a less experienced partner, you like to be in control, to be looked up to. It provides a partnership safe from critical commentary, but fraught with responsibility. You must teach your partner well to acquit yourself admirably. The key to your personality comes when this less experienced partner reaches your level. Will you join him in battle? Or will you release him to go on his way, so that you can start over again with another safe partner?

On the other hand, you may simply be a kind and generous person. You enjoy being a mentor and want to guide and develop a promising player. This often includes a cooperative effort with other members of your group who foresee a potential partner/team member. They will pitch in so that the responsibility doesn't fall on your shoulders alone.

If you prefer a more experienced partner you are able to submerge your ego for a purpose. You are open to learning, to new ideas, to bettering your game. You might also like the chance of winning more often!

If you seek a partner who is on a par with you, you enjoy the cooperative building effort you can have with a peer. You want a comfortable relationship which can grow and improve, or stay the same if you each so desire.

Of course you may begin with one of these preferences and switch as your game matures; this is a natural flow.

Committed or Swinger?
Do you play with different people, or prefer to stick with one steady partner?

You may be an extrovert who likes to socialize; you are flexible, and knowledgeable enough to play any convention card. You like to experience it all, and can play with just about anyone, anytime. At the same time you enjoy penciling in your favorite partner once a week so you can relax and play your own pet conventions.

Alternatively you may be a serious player who wants to build a game with a like-minded partner, or who simply likes a comfort level and wants a known quantity. Either way, don't get in a rut; consider playing with different partners periodically. It helps avoid bridge burnout, and pushes you to learn new conventions. As a side benefit, you get to know some of your fellow bridge players on a more personal level.

TOOLS
Conventions

Do you like a convention card filled to the hilt with no room to spare, or do you prefer a simple approach based on logic and partnership rapport? Do you like to change your card as new conventions which may be useful come to light, or do you prefer to keep your comfortable old card that feels like cozy slippers on a winter night? Do you like to experiment with conventions, or keep your faithful tried and trues? Do you research expert opinions on new conventions, or do you avoid these "fads," judging them guilty until proven innocent?

These preferences can be expressed as Science v. Simplicity. The scientist constantly experiments. Change is a natural element in his environment. The simplicist has done his experimenting and loves the ease of the known system. He conserves energy otherwise spent trying to remember the latest gadget and uses that energy to employ his talent and logic to greater advantage.

Sometimes even the scientist has had enough. I love my bidding tools but on more than one occasion my partner has heard me cry desperately, "Hey, wait a minute - I can only remember so much." Then too, some bids come up

no more than every other monsoon season. Those
are the extras I put on hold. But then that's
me. I guess I am half and half - a practical
scientist (or is it a scientific simplicist?).

Game Analysis
        Do you analyze your results in depth, or
do you prefer a quick on-site discussion with
your partner?

        If you are an intense student of the
game, you have ambition and a bit of an ego.
You want to know in detail where you went wrong
and what you did right. If you are a more
social player, you may just wish to have a good
time and keep your analysis brief. You want to
improve, but not to agonize over every hand.
You enjoy being a member of the club, like to
relax, and say "never mind" to all the drama.
You tend to be a thoughtful, fun partner who
doesn't indulge in recriminations.

TECHNIQUE
Bidding, Play of the Hand, and Defense
Do you see the FOREST or the TREES?

        Bidding - If this is your forte you like
detail, language, puzzles. You have
imagination. Your goal is to create a
meaningful dialogue with your partner. You see
each and every tree. Unfortunately, after the
bidding is over, you have to place the trees in
the forest.

        Need help with bidding? Don't miss Marty
Bergen's Points Schmoints! It will
revolutionize your bidding world, stretch your
parameters and leave you reeling. It will
point you toward bidding more accurately - and
more often! Once you get the basics down, try
Marty's Slam Bidding Made Easier. You'll amaze
even the pros.

        Play - If your dummy play is brilliant
you are analytical, goal oriented, and enjoy
being in charge. You immediately set a plan in
motion, yet are flexible enough to change

horses in mid-stream if necessary. You see the trees and can glimpse the forest. A mental helicopter is handy for those difficult times when the trees don't behave themselves as they should.

If this is your weak point, the old standard and acknowledged classic on dummy play is Louis H. Watson's Play of the Hand. It starts with basics, continues with advanced, then psychological play and technique. Keep this one in your bridge library. I have a battered copy on my own bookshelf.

How to Play a Bridge Hand by William S. Root is an ideal read for intermediate players. Root includes over 300 sample hands and provides a detailed analysis for each.

Defense - If you love to defend you are an "overall picture" person. You see the forest and the trees in one fell swoop. You listen, visualize, analyze, and count throughout the auction and play. You know when to regroup. You and your partner operate as a fearless SWAT team.

If you aren't quite swatting yet, try How to Defend a Bridge Hand by William S. Root. It covers everything.

I will digress with a bit of personal history. Defense used to be the worst part of my game. I couldn't seem to get it down. I was frantically frustrated. I decided to try Mike Lawrence's book, Dynamic Defense. It was an eye-opener. I found many of the "rules" I had learned were made to be broken - or at least made subject to thoughtful common sense. The book stresses working to see the WHOLE PICTURE. My defense began to improve. I started to think, rather than defend like Robert the Robot.

I realized I had the same problem in my personal life. I could see each and every tree but was missing the forest. I would hire an unknown handyman, believe every word he said, and fall in love with his low estimate. Would I check his references? No. Would I get referrals from my friends and neighbors? No. Was I happy with the results? No.

I opened my eyes wider. I envisioned not just a beginning, but an end result as well. Was I finally happy with the results? Yes!

This lesson inspired me to analyze all parts of my game and to relate them to my personality and habits. Wow. That mirror worked overtime for a while.

The Opening Lead

An old bridge adage advises when in doubt, lead the suit closest to your thumb. That is a stretch, but the math whizzes do claim a successful opening lead is due to pure chance roughly one-third of the time!

To make the best opening lead possible, or at least to avoid the worst lead, you need to listen patiently to the bidding. At the same time, try to visualize the distribution and strength of the various hands. If you are hyperactive, a daydreamer, or find it hard to construct a general picture from our limited bridge vocabulary, just do your best. Opening leads aren't a strict science. There are guidelines of course, but one's hand doesn't always fit the nice patterns the books present as examples.

A first-rate book to boost the accuracy of your opening leads is Opening Leads by Mike Lawrence. It's a fun, easy read and includes hundreds of example hands. You will soon know what to lead when, and why.

BRIDGE WORLD PARAMETERS
Game Venues

Do you play in club games, sectionals? Do you take on regionals, perhaps branch out to nationals?

You may prefer community level bridge and the social scene; the known is a comfortable certainty. You may want to extend yourself, be part of a bigger picture now and then. Getting outside the box can bring excitement and adventure and, win or lose, the thrill of competition in a larger field.

Age also factors into some of these decisions. Flying to a national in Toronto was great fun a few years ago, but today I am thinking DC is close enough (I live in Virginia).

Pairs or Teams?

Do you prefer to play in pairs events or team games?

If you like to take your future in your own hands, with a partner you trust, then you will gravitate to pairs events. If you like the challenge of choosing the perfect team and making a cooperative effort, you'll enter team events. Of course nowadays team games represent more points, so the greed factor can outweigh other considerations, especially if you are chasing that Life Master goal.

SELF ANALYSIS

You will think of many more examples. Look for them, be alert and aware. Ask yourself questions. What type of people do you associate with; what is your risk vs. comfort level; do you prefer one-on-one, or a group effort; do you see the forest or the trees; can you multi-task; are you using all the input available; do you learn from your results; do you learn from others; do you like to stay within comfortable parameters; do you like to experiment; do you like detail; are you easily bored; do you seek more efficient tools, disregarding a temporary setback; the list goes on...

You will learn a lot about yourself by analyzing your bridge game (or your golf, tennis or Scrabble game…). You may decide to try to see the forest a bit more often, or to extend yourself a bit now and then. You may decide you are quite happy with the way you are and leave it at that. The choice, as always, is entirely your own. After all, if it ain't broke, you don't have to fix it - but that doesn't mean you can't polish it up a little!

The final word is, have fun, have fun, and have more fun.

"Nothing reveals so much about us as how we play the games we play." - Q, Star Trek.

***

TOURNAMENT FEVER

I get up at dawn,
Snatch my coffee cup,
Dash to the site,
Round my teammates up.

I part with some cash,
And look for our place,
We make all the boards,
And begin the race.

The caffeine kicks in;
I'm feeling alive.
But my high starts to fade
When I go down five...

I drown my sorrows
In a beer, at break,
While partner lectures,
In hopes I'll go straight.

Things pick up at last -
There's a chance for first place;
Even sourpuss partner
Has a smile on his face.

Bam! It's over, we've won!
We revel in glory.
I replay the battle,
Telling many a story.

Exhausted and worn,
I fall into bed;
Visions of bridge hands
Still clog up my head.

Yet *is* it over?
We've hardly begun;
Tomorrow comes soon,
With the rise of the sun...

"It's always the challenge of the future, this feeling of excitement, that drives me." - *Yoshihisa Tabuchi.*

KEEP YOUR EYE ON THE GOLD

"To him, battles were an inspiration, a challenge, exciting, and a Hell of a lot of fun." General Eisenhower describing General George Patton.

Tournament bridge is not for the faint of heart - or body. Stress and tension runs high. You burn a lot of mental and physical energy. Stamina is king. It is crucial to remain alert and keep your focus. You need to make the best judgment calls and play your cards like an expert. Whew! How can you manage all this, have fun, and still be alive for the next session?

STRATEGIC PLANNING
Pre-Tournament
"Practice makes perfect." - Proverb.

Training starts prior to the tournament - and not just a day or two prior, mind you. You want to be certain that, in the heat of battle, you can instantly summon to mind all of your conventions and agreements. This keeps your brain cells from going into overdrive, possibly exploding. It also keeps your partner from going into overdrive, possibly exploding.

Toward this end you must study, practice, review, practice, memorize, and practice. Your partnership agreements must become so ingrained that recall of your entire system is automatic. This saves time, relieves you of stress, and rescues you from malevolent glares from partner. It leaves energy to deal with any curve balls the opponents throw your way.

The night before the tournament get plenty of sleep. Don't go out on the town, don't get into a fight with your spouse, don't do your taxes. Wake up refreshed and ready to GO. Give yourself plenty of time to get ready.

Arrive at the site early. Find the playing area, greet your partner, and get your entry; no rushing about, burning up your precious energy on anything other than bridge.

The Day Arrives
"My soul is dark with stormy riot, directly traceable to diet." - Samuel Hoffenstein.

A vital part of pre-game strategy involves food. Be finished eating at least one hour prior to game time. Otherwise your brain will compete with your stomach. Your stomach will win. Once the body is alerted to all those biscuits and gravy waiting to be broken down, the flow of oxygen, so instrumental to clarity of thought, will instead go toward digestion.

If you know you get hungry mid-way through the session, bring along a pick-me-up snack of fruit or nuts. You notice I did not mention doughnuts or candy bars. Fruits boost and sustain energy. Sweets give you a brief kick but before long actually *rob* you of energy, rendering you apathetic and lifeless. You will note later this dip in energy occurred at the same time you entered a few bottoms on your scorecard. Yuck.

I confess that I'm a "grazer," and must have a bite of something, anything, at a moment's notice. I bring a special tote bag dedicated to snacks to every tournament. I know I'll be approached to share so I bring plenty. Running out is not an option - I do not play well hungry. Further, as my partner will attest, I'm not a nice person when I'm hungry...grrrr.

Break Time
"The belly rules the mind." - Spanish Proverb.

At the break between sessions eat early and light. This gives your food time to digest and once more keeps oxygen flowing in the right direction. When I see my opponents nodding off I know they had the Combination Plate at El Taco.

My partner and I like to split an entrée. This keeps both the amount of food and the cost down. We never walk away hungry. There have been times when I was aghast at the tiny portion on my plate, but with salad, rolls, and chewing slowly my stomach was content.

Keep conversation upbeat. To go over hands from the prior session, to moan over errors and disasters, only raises your blood pressure and expends valuable energy. It doesn't make your partner feel too kindly toward you either, which never bodes well for the upcoming session.

During the Session
"Energy and persistence conquer all things." - Benjamin Franklin.

Imagine all your energy for the day is in an internal "gas tank". That one fill-up is it. You have to get great gas mileage to survive.

When you are in the thick of things, with those 13 cards in your hands, use down time to relax. Don't watch partner play the hand. Conserve your mental energy for the next board. This will also keep at bay the ever-present temptation to interject observations of partner's technique. You may be a genius, but partners do not always appreciate hearing Einstein's theories. Unless of course you are extolling his expertise in glowing terms.

At game's end the hand records can be used to discuss pertinent points and useful lessons. This will keep the energy of the partnership flowing in a positive direction and toward a common goal - the Gold.

If, in spite of all efforts, your energy lags or your concentration wanders, get some coffee, walk around at the break, pop a raisin or two. Give yourself a pep talk. Put an ice cube down your back. Recognize the symptoms and take *action*.

As always, there will be situations you just can't control. You will be fixed by a pair of innocent looking LOL's (Little Old Ladies), or by chance, or by your own greed. Which reminds me of a hand...

```
Dlr: S                    J109
Vul:  E/W                 10xx
                          xxx
                          Qxxx
              AKxxxx                  Qx
              AKQJxx                  9xxx
              A                       xxx
              ---                     xxxx
                          xx
                          ---
                          KQJ10xx
                          AKJ10x
```

We are playing a team game, against a pair of sweet senior ladies. I am South. The bidding goes as follows:

West	North	East	South
			1D
6H	P	P	7C (I'll show them)
P	P	7H !!	X (How dare they)
P	P	P	

As you can see, there is no way our opponents can avoid making 7H, doubled. Minus 2170 points later, our heads were reeling. I asked my right hand opponent what in the world made her bid 7. She told me that her partner never bids 6, so she knew that they must be able to make 7! There went our match. To add salt to the wound, we couldn't avoid reliving this fiasco all day long; our opponents loved repeating it to anyone within hearing distance.

RESULTS

"It does not matter how slowly you go so long as you do not stop." - Confucius.

So after all your efforts you may end up with Silver, Bronze, perhaps honorable mention. You may (shudder) not even scratch. Don't get discouraged. Keep in training. There is always the next time. And the next. True bridge champs *never* give up.

GOLD is waiting for you.

"Failure is more frequently from want of energy than want of capital." - Daniel Webster.

* * *

THE UNKNOWN QUANTITY

"A pessimist sees the difficulty in every opportunity; an optimist sees the opportunity in every difficulty." - Winston Churchill.

You decide to try out the new restaurant in town. You've heard the food is gourmet and the service impeccable. Your sources have good taste. You arrive, and enter. Lights glitter, crystal sparkles, marvelous aromas mingle. You are approaching an unknown quantity, but you are excited, and have high hopes.

You buy a new book. You don't know the author, but it got rave reviews. Several of your friends have said it is a must. Of course, everyone's taste differs. But the story-line sounds intriguing and the few paragraphs you have scanned left you wanting more. It is an unknown quantity, but you are excited and have high hopes.

You are unexpectedly freed from a business meeting in Nebraska. You are disappointed, but can now catch a local tournament. You arrive at the partnership desk to seek out a partner. The partnership chairman is delighted, as he has the perfect match for you. He outlines her stats in glowing terms. You see a bouncy redhead with a big smile coming toward you. She is an unknown quantity. But you are excited, and you have high hopes.

Your high hopes may or may not be realized, but the anticipation, the excitement, leads you toward adventure and a new experience. You are open and have a positive mind-set. This always sets the stage for an interesting result.

In the bridge world, picking up a partner continues with the dance of the cards - the

convention cards, that is. Your first
agreement should be to *KEEP IT SIMPLE*. With an
unknown partner, you want to minimize risks.
Forget your favorite "two-way multi-level
upside-down monkey wrench" convention. Agree
to play anything that you are both familiar
with, and go standard with all else. Don't get
stubborn and insist on odd/even if your partner
usually plays standard. Your partner will
forget, be frustrated, and feel like kicking
you under the table. This usually does not
bode well for the immediate future. Agree that
if either of you are not certain about whether
a bid is forcing, you will treat it as forcing.
Best to err on the side of optimism. Discuss
in detail the conventions you do agree to play.
"Let's play Drury," just doesn't cut it. After
all, there is reverse, two-way, even upside-
down Drury (and who knows what else lurks in
the mind of man – The Shadow knows, but he
isn't playing bridge).

Following the "simple" formula, I have
had great success with pickup partners. I find
many other players have also had good results.
I once picked up a partner with whom I
continued to play for five years. My high
hopes had been exceeded.

Why does this so often work? It is the
ever-present human element. When meeting
someone new, we want to make a good impression.
We want the person to think we are "with it".
We are clear and concise so that there will be
no misunderstandings. We stay focused. With a
new partner, we work especially hard to
establish good rapport and to be flexible and
reliable. This positive attitude and state of
mental alertness invariably enhances our game.
Now why do we not carry all of this over to our
regular partnership? We are so (yawn) used to
our steady partner that we sometimes take him
for granted. We get a little sloppy, a little
relaxed. We may even be wondering what to have

for dinner in the middle of an auction.
Naughty, naughty.

But back to our pickup partner. We each
so want to sparkle, to outshine the other, that
we both play at the top of our game. We
discuss without rancor because, after all, this
is our first time playing together. We can't
possibly be expected to read the other's mind,
to do everything just right. As long as we
have been well-paired, and are on a par, this
situation presents the potential for a maximum
result. Whatever the outcome, neither of us
can feel too bad about it, and if all has gone
well, we will pat each other on the back.
Maybe even give a "yahoo" or two.

I recall a time when my partner and I
picked up a pair for a Swiss team. We asked
about their points, and they told us 1,000. We
didn't realize at the time that they meant
1,000 between the two of them. We did not do
well, but they were eager and earnest. After
the game, I went for coffee. When I returned,
my partner had agreed to play in the BAMs with
them. I can't leave her alone for a minute.
She explained that they were most sorry, but
had ironed out all their problems (in the space
of 3 hours) and were sure they would do better
this time. What could I do? I took a deep
breath, and said to myself, "Okay, Self, be
excited and have high hopes." Didn't we just
win. Our reincarnated pair were ecstatic. Of
course, so were we.

Sometimes we get a little too picky. I
heard this story from a partnership desk
volunteer. A mother who was mentoring her
daughter dropped her off for a partner in the
side game, thinking a tournament experience
would help spur her on. The poor girl
approached the desk with trepidation, and
confessed, "I think you might have a hard time
finding someone, because I only have one

masterpoint." She was assured they would try. A short time later a man came up to the desk for a partner, but advised he as yet had no points at all. The partnership chairman called the young lady over. "What!" she exclaimed. "No points at all? I'll wait."

It's a shame that we often seem to shun the partnership desk. It presents an opportunity for a bit of a gamble, the chance for a fun, relaxed game. The risk/reward factor is pretty much a free ride. Cast your fears to the wind. When, at the last minute, you have the option to participate in a tournament, stride right up to the partnership desk with excitement, and high hopes. They may just be realized.

"Twenty years from now, you will be more disappointed by the things you did not do than by the things you did do. So, throw off the bow lines. Sail away from the safe harbor. Catch the trade winds in your sails. Explore. Dream. Discover." - Mark Twain.

***

STRATEGY

MATCH POINTS

"What's the use of running if you are not on the right road? – German Proverb.

But we set them 1100! Why didn't we get a good score?

They only made 110 – why should they get a top?

We hear these common cries after a game at the club. Looking back at the printout, we see that in the first instance the opponents talked us out of a vulnerable slam which would have scored 1430. In the second, where the opponents were at 2H making, we could compete and make 2S, for a plus score instead of a minus. If the opponents then go on to bid 3H, they will go down, and we again get a plus score.

Match point scoring doesn't follow the rules of most other games we play. You don't necessarily need to get a big score. Your score is compared with the score of all other pairs holding your same cards on each deal. It doesn't matter by how much or by how little you beat the opponents' score, just whether you beat it, or not. It is this method of comparison scoring that affects all your match point decisions.

To Double or Not to Double. Let's look at a hand where a part-score battle is in progress:

All vulnerable, North deals. You (West)
hold:

KJ10   AKxxx   K107   xx

The bidding has gone:

North	East	South	West
P	P	P	1H
1S	X (neg.)	2S	P
P	3H	P	P
3S	P	P	?

Strategic thoughts float through your
mind – hopefully in quick succession. Some
lucky pairs in your position will be permitted
to play in 2 or 3H, making +110 or +140.
(Don't you just love silent opponents?) Even
if you defeat 3S one trick, +100 is not going
to look good on that score sheet. Your only
hope for a positive result is to *double*, trying
for +200. Whip out that red "X" card like you
mean it.

Play and Defense. Every trick counts.
As declarer, overtricks are prime. It's often
not enough just to make your contract if you
want a good score. Of course, if you feel
other pairs will not bid the aggressive game
your partner has pushed for, by all means take
no chances. Make the contract. Go plus. As
defender, the concept is the same. You don't
want to take undue risks on defense, giving
declarer an overtrick. As you can see, this
means playing a tight game. Any lapse in
concentration can be fatal.

If you are playing 24 boards you are in
reality playing 24 separate games. The result
of each contest will become part of your
overall score. Each hand is equal in terms of

importance, regardless of the contract - from a pass-out to a slam. Total attention to *each* hand is crucial for maximum results. Stamina is king.

Bidding

Wild West gamblers, step up. Stakes are high. Push, bluff, go for the gusto. Make war, not peace. Tempt your opponents to go one step beyond safety - then retreat, and take your plus. Going plus a majority of the time will give you good results a majority of the time.

Strike the first blow - the opponents will be stymied, make mistakes, be unsure of their footing. Super-sound opening bidding systems delight opponents - now *they* can strike the first blow.

When the other side opens, give them something to think about. Grab a card from the bidding box as though you have the world in your hand. This strategy invites your partner to compete, if feasible, and is valuable on defense when you have to bow out.

Are you aggressive enough? Do some research. How do you fare on part-score deals? Does your partnership usually play more hands than the average? If you are playing less than 55% of the hands you are mousy-meek, and even worse, cooperating with the enemy! Get excited, pump up your blood pressure, and start growling. It's a jungle out there.

Now about those vital part-score deals. "Why," you say, "do you keep going on about measly part-scores? I like games and slams." So do I, but part-scores make up about one-third of a duplicate game. If you treat them as insignificant, you risk getting milquetoast scores 33% of the time. Not a winning strategy. Competition for part-scores can be fierce. Each side pushes and pulls, grunts and groans, until the inevitable sigh and pass. Who has won? Let's see how it works.

You win if you have: 1) bid and made a part-score; 2) given up a small set; 3) pushed the opponents too high; 4) taken up bidding space so as to cramp your opponents' style; 5) communicated information to assist on defense if the opposition plays the hand. You accomplish this by bullying your opponents until your risk threatens to overcome your reward. Then you let them work their way out of the spider web.

Majors, Minors, or NT? "Oh, I know all about this," you declare. "The majors or NT are the only way to go because they score more points!" Well, they sure do, if you make your contract…

A big part of your decision depends on whether you are playing in a part-score, game, or slam.

If it is evident you don't have game, *safety* should be your goal. Remember, you want to **go plus**. Frequently, a good minor suit fit will be your only shot, and often outscores those NT lovers. Suit contracts regularly play a trick or two better than NT, especially when your hand is limited to a part-score.

When you have a game-going hand, your thinking changes. Now you know most of your competition will be going plus. You want to out-plus your opponents. "This is easy," you say. "Just bid NT." Hmmm. It may surprise you to find out that statistically, suit contracts play better than NT! If you have a combined 8+ card major suit fit, go with the flow and bid your major suit game. Of course, lacking a major fit, live it up, bid 3NT. Don't, however, completely overlook those lowly

108

minors. Sometimes they can be major players.
If your scientific bidding shows you have no
major fit, one suit is wide open, but you and
partner have 9 diamonds between you, take a
deep breath and bid 5D. When you make this
contract while those NTer's are going down,
take a bow – and your top as well. You have
just out-plussed your opponents.

We come to slams, our favorite contracts.
"Now can I bid NT?" you plaintively inquire.
That NT must have a big ego. It always seems
to be in demand. Once again, safety becomes an
important issue. Keep slam tries below the
level of game if possible. It would be a shame
to go down at the 5 level while others are
making game. If, however, you discover you do
have a slam, avoid the trap of going for a few
more match points by bidding a doubtful major
or your buddy NT. Simply reaching and making a
slam is statistically worth 75-80% of the match
points on any board. So play in the *safest*
slam. "Gee whiz, not again," you moan. Yes,
again. Remember, even in a strong field, good
slams are missed by many pairs. Be sure you
make yours. Of course, sometimes you will have
such an overabundance of strength that you know
everyone will be in slam. Only THEN is it ever
advisable to think about skipping over your
safe suit-fit, and bidding NT. "Yes! Finally,"
you cheer. As to grand slams, you must be
absolutely certain that 13 tricks are there,
regardless of 5-0 splits. It is not worth
giving up a small slam to bid an iffy grand
slam. If you are not *totally* sure, give it up.

When to Double. There are three types of
doubles that are vital to match point strategy.

1.   You have the big guns. You know
(i) you will gain more points defending than
playing the hand; or (ii) their sacrifice is
going down, *and* you can't safely bid one more.
Opponents can be so inconsiderate.

2. Your opponents are in trouble and don't know it. Your hand shows distribution is against them, and, you hold key high cards in an advantageous position. In other words, they will lose a critical finesse, or two. You are confident that (i) they cannot run to another contract, and (ii) other pairs holding the same cards will reach the same contract. Just going plus will be very average. How boring. Time for *you* to be inconsiderate. You will take nothing less than a super-plus.

3. You want an unusual lead. You expect to defeat the opponents big-time, or even better, defeat an otherwise iron-clad contract. Be sure you and partner are on the same wave-length, however. Otherwise, OUCH.

Sacrifices. Again, match point scoring dictates action. Losing 500 points when the opponents can make 620, or even 1100 when they have a vulnerable slam for 1400, can give you a top board. Then too, the opponents, knowing this will be a bad board for them, may bid one level higher, and go down. You will love this. Now you are *assured* of a top board. Or at least tied for top, if another pair in your direction is as bold as your partnership.

Do not sacrifice (i) if you have a chance of setting the contract; (ii) if you feel most pairs won't bid game or slam; (iii) if there is a possibility your sacrifice will go down more than your opponents would score; or (iv) if there is a chance your opponents might make the contract should they go one level higher, say from a small to a grand slam. You have traded an average for a bottom. Yuck.

Listen carefully to the auction. If you feel your opponents have struggled to get to their game or slam, never mind the save. They might not make it, and your post-mortem will be a bit embarrassing.

When the opponents have bid 7, it is logical that other pairs will bid at least 6. In this situation a sacrifice can bring you glory, especially if you go down less than the value of a small slam.

Sometimes your strategy won't work out. You will get caught in a competitive whirlpool and go down when your wimpy opponents don't take the push. Your enemies will make a doubled contract. Your sacrifice will be a flop. "Oh, I knew I shouldn't have listened to that advice," you will declare petulantly. "I'm going to pare back and play it safe." Now, now. Do not let these setbacks turn you into jello. Statistics don't lie. You've got to take a few falls now and then. Overall, your calculated aggressive actions will pay off. You will win more often and become a feared opponent. "Oh, oh," your opponents will say. "Here come those doubling fools. We'd better play it close to the chest." You'll have an advantage before you even reach the table.

Know your game, know yourself, know your opponents. Use the right strategy at the right time. You will be a full-time winner.

"Have a plan. Follow the plan, and you'll be surprised how successful you can be..." – Paul "Bear" Bryant.

* * *

STRATEGY

IMPS/SWISS TEAMS

*"Would you tell me which way I ought to go from
here?" asked Alice.
"That depends a good deal on where you want to
get," said the Cat.
"I really don't care where," replied Alice.
"Then it doesn't much matter which way you go,"
said the Cat. - Lewis Carroll.*

Fortunately, we bridge players care where
we're going, so we seek directions at every
turn. In this instance, we are inquiring into
the difference in strategy between MP and IMP
play.

IMPS scoring is unique - quite a
different animal from match points. Your
strategic mind set must change when you go into
battle in a team game. Set aside those tactics
you learned for a pairs challenge, and change
gears. At IMPS, you will have only *one* set of
opponents, not the multiple pairs who hold your
same cards at match points.

Even at IMPS scoring, there is a
difference in strategy depending on whether you
are in a long IMP match, as when you play in a
stratified team game, or are playing in the
usual 7-board Swiss Team match. In a long
match an early disaster or dramatic success
should not affect your action on the next deal.
There is time to even things out. In a short
Swiss match a disaster might tempt you to swing
on the next appropriate board.

Success at match points is defined by how
often, not by how much, you outscore your
opponents. The key to winning IMPS is by how
much, not by how often, you beat the
opposition. Also, you have only one set of
opponents to contend with at IMPS, rather than

a whole field. At match points, a 1D contract
is as important as a 6NT contract; IMP scoring
doesn't see it that way. At match points, an
overtrick may get you a top. At IMPS, an
overtrick is not, ever, worth more than 1 IMP.
At match points, the point difference for
majors, minors and no trump can be decisive; at
IMP scoring it makes very little difference.

International Match Point Scale

Point Spread	Imps Won	Point Spread	Imps Won	Point Spread	Imps Won
20-40	1	370- 420	9	1500-1740	17
50-60	2	430- 490	10	1750-1990	18
90-120	3	500- 590	11	2000-2240	19
130-160	4	600- 740	12	2250-2490	20
170-210	5	750- 890	13	2500-2990	21
220-260	6	900- 1090	14	3000-3490	22
270-310	7	1100-1290	15	3500-3990	23
320-360	8	1300-1490	16	4000 +	24

Declarer Beware

No fireworks, no high-wire acts. SAFETY
SAFETY SAFETY. Go plus. Make that contract.
Extra tricks are fluff, unless you can get them
without risking your contract *in any way*.

Game Anyone?

Should you bid a close game? Check out
the vulnerability. The odds are about even
when considering a close *non-vulnerable* game.
A close *vulnerable* game, however, gives you 10-
6 odds. As you can see, it is best, within
reason, to bid any close vulnerable game. Bid
a non-vulnerable game only when you are
confident you can make it.

Is It Slam Time?

IMPS odds change with small slams. Vulnerability is no longer a factor. Your opponents' style, however, is. If you know they are very aggressive bidders, this may color your actions. The greater percentage of the time, however, close slams will not be bid at the other table. If you are ahead in a Swiss match, or playing a weaker team, be a conservative. If you are the underdog, or are behind, play for a big swing and bid that close slam. It may win you the match.

Odds against grand slams are considerable. They are made worse when you consider that your opponents may have a misunderstanding and stop at game. At that point you have lost 26 IMPS if you go down in a vulnerable grand. That's a lot to make up. In addition, it is rare to see grand slams bid at teams, so a small slam is likely to at least be a "push" board. The experts advise never to bid a grand slam unless you can absolutely positively for sure count all 13 tricks. You might find it hard to believe that your opponents will miss a small slam when you are looking for a grand slam, but records show that it happens fairly often. Do not risk a Titanic result by bidding a squeaky grand slam unless you feel your team is going to sink anyway.

Don't Sweat the Small Stuff

A small one or two IMP loss on any one deal is usually no big deal at Swiss teams. The difference between making +90 in 2-D, or scoring +120 in NT, can be disastrous at match points, but makes little difference at teams. Setting the opponents for +100 when you could have made +140 by declaring in 3H is only a one IMP difference. The real secret to winning Swiss teams is to get a *plus* score on the small hands. If you and your teammates can get plus scores on the majority of part-score hands, you will win the majority of the matches you play.

Unlike match points, your ultimate goal is
simply to go plus. Don't be concerned about
getting a big plus, or a small minus. Just go
plus. As declarer you are willing to risk
going down two instead of one if it gives you a
chance to make your contract. By the same
token, you must not risk your contract for an
overtrick. Take those safety plays and get
that plus.

As defender, you can get creative.
Visualize what partner can have to help you set
the contract. Don't worry one bit about giving
the opponents an overtrick if you have a
reasonable chance to set the contract. No need
to indulge in wishful thinking, however. If
the bidding has told you that partner cannot
possibly hold the card you need, no reason to
give the opponents an extra IMP or two. Just
play your usual tight defense.

As you can see, the strategy at IMPS is
to make, or set, contracts.

Part-Score Battles
        IMPS does mirror MPs when it comes to
fighting for part-scores. Don't let your
opponents rest easy at the two-level if you can
avoid it. When your partners make a part-score
at the other table, and you set your opponents
one when they go down at the three-level, you
pick up 5 IMPS. This isn't to be sneezed at,
especially in a short Swiss Team match – it
could bump you right into the lead.

        A good rule of thumb when in a skirmish
over a part-score: Push the opposition to the
three-level, then go for that precious plus.

A Sacrificial Lamb?
        "Should I lay myself on those railroad
tracks for the good of the team?" you might
wonder.

116

At match points, taking a -300 point hit when your opponents are making +420 is a great result. At Swiss Teams you save only 3 IMPS. If there is any chance you can defeat the opposition's game, go for that result instead. The death knell tolls when you sacrifice against an *unmakable* game. Let's say you go down 500 when those brassy opponents would have gone down one. Now you lose 12 IMPS. When your excellent partners at the other table have judiciously stayed out of game, ouch. Not a postmortem I'd like to attend.

Then, too, the possibility of pushing your opponents one level higher at IMPS is not likely. They will be much more inclined to double. They don't have as much to lose vs. the same situation at MPs.

Regardless of all these dire warnings, it always benefits to sacrifice 100 or 300 points against a vulnerable game, anytime, anywhere. By the same token, it pays to take the push to the 5 level when you feel you can make your bid, rather than let the thieving opponents steal your game and get by with going down just one. You may hear generic advice admonishing, "Do Not Sacrifice," and "Double all Saves". Never pay attention to advisors who are always saying "never" or "always".

The advance save can also be used to great advantage. This sacrifice catapults the opponents to the 5 level before they are ready. You are so devious! They then have to guess. They may take the push and go down. They may miss a slam. Even if they guess correctly, your sacrifice may make money. This tactic aims at a 12 IMP gain. Let's say your partner, at favorable vulnerability, opens 3C. Your right hand opponent doubles. Your hand is:

```
          6
        AJ9
        QJ962
        K973
```

Jump to 5C immediately. Make your opponents
sweat a little.

       Sacrifices against slams frequently save
a lot of IMPS, especially when vulnerability is
favorable and you have a fit. If you are down
6, doubled, for -1100, your team gains 8 IMPS
when your partners are plus 1430. Yes! This
works against grand slams as well. There are,
however, two warnings. If there is a
possibility the enemy's slam will go down, or
that your partners may not bid slam, pass, and
hope that you are especially inspired on
defense.

To Double or Not to Double
       When considering a close penalty double
at IMPS, the word is - DON'T. In a team match
you are not competing against a field. If your
opponents have stumbled and bumbled into game,
they will probably go down. But there is such
a thing as luck. If your opponent's contract
is iffy, your partners probably are making a
part-score, so you don't want to tip the
scales. A good result will suffice.

       Unless you are absolutely positively
totally sure that your opponents are going
down, *do not double part-scores at IMPS*. If
you have three aces and a holding such as
QJ1098 in the opponents' suit, you might think
about it. A good rule of thumb is to ask
yourself, "Can we set them at least two?"

       Lead-directing doubles can be a good bet
at IMPS, much more so than at MPs. If the lead
gives declarer an overtrick, no big deal at
IMPS. The odds makers give an 11-4 edge to a
well-advised directional double of a game

contract. Just make sure you and your partner
discuss what these doubles mean before you get
into the fray. The odds change when you don't
both know what is being said.

A shaky slam contract presents an even
more appealing opportunity for a lead-directing
double. If your teammates make game while your
opponents make their non-vulnerable slam, your
loss from doubling the slam is 1 IMP. When
your double defeats the slam, your team gains
22 IMPS (a gain of 11 as opposed to a loss of
11). These odds of 22-1 encourage a good lead-
directing double.

Strategy in a Nutshell
Your goals at Swiss Teams differ greatly
from those at MPs. You only have to beat one
team at a time. If you get everything that
belongs to you without going after what belongs
to your opponents, you will win most Swiss
matches. The key is to avoid bloopers. Know
your system inside and out, and discuss your
strategy. A mutual 51% game insures a win.
That score at MPs would do you no good at all.

Special Swiss Team Considerations
Know your opponents. Are they advanced,
intermediate, or beginners? Where does your
team stand in relation to your opponents?

If your team is by far the more
experienced, all team members should play their
customary solid game. Don't take chances. Let
your opponents lose the match all by
themselves. A bad result should not induce you
to go crazy on the next board. Your poor
result may be reproduced at the other table, or
your partners may make up for it on their own.

If you are playing a team that is on a
par with you, again, play your typical tight
game. Maintain your concentration and avoid
sloppy mistakes. Analyze each board. If you

have a disaster early on, be aggressive. If
you get lucky at the start, register
Republican.

If you come up against an expert buzz
saw, you can be freewheeling. Now you will
show your liberal colors. Bid close games and
slams. Compete like a bulldog in those part-
score auctions. Your opponents will be playing
it cool, since they have the upper hand. They
undoubtedly can play and defend like demons, so
your best shot at winning will be to outbid
them. This does not mean to use kamikaze
tactics. You want to survive, not go down with
the ship. Watch for opportunities to be
aggressive - preempt freely, and compete early
and often.

It's Not the 4th of July

Regardless of outcome, put the postmortem
fireworks on hold. Team rapport is crucial.
Built-up steam sidetracks a teammate from
giving full concentration to each board. His
attention fades as he uses his mental energy to
plan appropriate barbs and comebacks to the
deluge of criticism which he perceives as
unwarranted. Besides, next time it might be
your turn. Be understanding, discuss ways to
avoid similar problems in the future, and move
on.

Strategy Ambassador

Now that you know all about IMP strategy,
you can educate your teammates in time for your
next tournament. Put together a little crib
sheet for review between bouts. An ounce of
prevention is worth a pound of cure, and
usually also worth a win or two.

*"Before beginning, plan carefully." - Marcus T.
Cicero.*

***

THE SUMMER NATIONALS
WASHINGTON D.C.
July 2009

"Life is either a daring adventure or it is nothing." - Helen Keller.

The Nationals. It has a ring to it. It is excitement, adventure, big points, huge crowds, star gazing. It is thousands of bridge players babbling about systems, bids, hands, fixes, tops, their beloved partners (clearly at fault for all bottoms). It is bridge heaven.

My partner and I ventured forth with long-lived anticipation to the 2009 Summer Nationals. We had relished this moment all year.

The reputation of these tournaments is well deserved, and did not disappoint us in D.C. The site (the Marriott Wardman Park Hotel) was spectacular. One of the playing rooms, ONE mind you, was four times the size of my house. The hotel could accommodate more people than the entire population (approximately 35,000) of Gloucester County, Virginia, my home base. Since I am totally without a directional guide in my brain, I was terrified to go from one end of the hotel to the other without my partner serving as a GPS. I am *not* kidding.

Everything proceeded smoothly. Games were efficiently run and experienced directors were in abundance. Volunteers were everywhere to guide, answer questions, and hand out Daily Bulletins. Mind-bending mini-lessons and lectures were presented by national experts. There was the hospitality (translation, food) that we have each come to expect. All of this takes on the air of a miracle when you consider that over the 11 day period of the tournament a total of 14,115 tables were in play.

The only glitch occurred when the government marched in just a few weeks prior to the tournament. Officials informed the hotel it was required to dedicate two entire floors to a special Chinese delegation! The hotel had signed a contract for this Summer National seven years in advance, and accepted reservations for many of these rooms. Bridge players were offered rooms in one of the hotel's satellite locations, at a reduced rate. Shuttles were provided. It was an inconvenience, but the hotel worked frantically to provide the best possible solution. It certainly didn't dampen enthusiasm and gave us all something to discuss-and-cuss about. For the first time in history political conversation prevailed at a bridge tournament.

Of course all the big names were there. We ran into Cappelletti Sr., Mike Lawrence, Jeff Meckstroth and Eric Rodwell, Zia Mahmood, Larry Cohen … the list goes on. One early morning we spotted Zia, erect and self-confident, taking long strides through the lobby in a flowing white tunic. He cut quite a figure. I understand the tunic is an element of dress in his native Pakistan. During game time, Zia was dressed in his well-known cosmopolitan manner.

Next day, as my partner and I settled in to play, we once again discovered Zia, playing with a beautiful, glamorous woman. Our minds immediately began speculating. Was this his girlfriend, his daughter, a client? We later learned, to our great chagrin, that the other player was Sabine Zenkel Auken, an expert of international reputation from Denmark. We, who think of ourselves as enlightened women, had never even given a thought to the fact that they may have been players of equal status who had made plans to play together in the Nationals for their mutual benefit.

Between sessions, of course, one must
eat. There was absolutely no way you could go
hungry. You could eat at the hotel. You could
easily walk - in balmy weather - to one of
hundreds of restaurants within reach of the
hotel, all offering choice delights. It was
phenomenal.

While we waited for a table at our
favorite deli, I checked out the area. Within
a block were the Mexican Grill, Indian Punjab,
Mr. Chen's Chinese Cuisine, and Baskin Robbins.
Next door was an Irish Pub. If you couldn't
find what you wanted, you were probably an
Eskimo craving whale blubber.

We even took an adventurous turn and
tried some Afghani food. Although a bit leery,
we decided we might not get another chance
(there certainly aren't any Afghani restaurants
in Gloucester). We went boldly up the stairs,
as directed, and edged open the door.
Immediate enchantment took us by surprise.
White gleaming walls were accented by brilliant
photographs taken by Steve McCurry. Exotic
hints of mint, saffron and coriander quickened
our senses. The owner proudly led us to a
table set with linen, silver and crystal. We
sampled happy dishes of lamb and rice,
eggplant, dumplings, fried sweet potatoes and
yogurt cheese. Another great memory.

A personal highlight came when my article
"Successful Partnerships" was published in the
National's "Daily Bulletin." Win or lose, my
day was made. I asked one of the volunteers
passing out bulletins for 10 of them. He
smiled. "You must have an article in today."
I grinned sheepishly.

It was over all too soon. We checked out
with a sigh and made ready to return to the
real world. We had spent a lot of money, taken

on a few more calories than needed, and
experienced an amazing, memorable, fun fun
time. If you've never been to a National, do
not let anyone deter you. Once may be enough,
but it is an experience you will prize. I
always say I am not going again, but I always
go again. And again.

"*Plunge boldly into the thick of life, and
seize it where you will, it is always
interesting.*" - *Goethe*.

***

ARE YOU SUFFERING FROM BBO?

"Burnout is nature's way of telling you, you've been going through the motions, your soul has departed, you're a zombie..." - Sam Keen.

I picked up the phone. My heart sunk. "Oh Pard," I heard. "We simply must allow at least three days for Richmond, I can book a room, no problem. We need to leave early so we can get lunch, get settled, and … blah blah blah." I barely heard the words. I mumbled something, said how wonderful it was for her to take care of everything, and rang off. I tried to go back to my book, but the walls started closing in. I felt short of breath. My mind was whirling. A million voices sounded in my head. I threw the book down and rushed out of the house. I needed air.

* * *

BBO strikes when you least expect it. Of all bridge diseases it is the most dreaded. "It will never get me," you vow. *"Impossible."* I felt the same way. Then, out of the blue, it hit me - Bridge Burn Out!

The Signs
What are the symptoms of this horrible virus? Ask yourself these questions: Are you becoming bored with the game? Are you crabby with your partner (more than usual)? Do you play a scheduled game out of duty? Do you feel a certain malaise, can't seem to concentrate? Is the most exciting thing at a tournament the food? Are five days of playing bridge JUST TOO MUCH?

The Causes
Sometimes, with our hectic lifestyles, family responsibilities, and the stress of everyday living, we start to feel closed in, overwhelmed. The simplest thing can be that final straw (like when partner trumps your Ace

- *twice*). That's when you need to regroup, relax, and relieve the built-up pressure.

Fighting it Off
Involve Your Partner
If you have a steady partner, you will need her help and support. Explain what you're going through. She undoubtedly will have noticed changes in your game and personality. My partner thought I had some kind of dementia. She might have been right.

Outline your strategy. You don't want your partner to feel left out, alone, abandoned. Let her know that you'll be back in the swing of things soon.

BBO is sometimes encouraged when partners take each other for granted. They may berate and accuse, glare and glower. "Tactful" drops from their vocabulary. Going through BBO therapy often brings a partnership back to balance and equanimity.

Gear Down
I began my recovery by scheduling fewer club games. I restricted sectional commitments to two days.

I played relaxed on-line games with pick-up partners. I stepped out of my box. I agreed to play unknown partner's card, even when I thought his conventions came from outer space. I nicknamed one particularly convoluted contraption the "Pluto" convention.

Make it Fun Again
It helps to revitalize if you read a good bridge book (Mike Lawrence and Marty Bergen write fun, easy, helpful books). An expert author can boost your game and expand your horizons.

Try a new convention. It can be exciting to stretch yourself and learn new things. If you and your partner are trying something new there will be more discussion and less squabbling.

Play with different partners periodically. If nothing else it may help you better appreciate your regular partner. Play in different clubs, expand your horizons, meet new people.

Take lessons from an expert or from an experienced player in your local club. Get that adrenaline pumping once more.

Tournaments
Give your mind a rest - break up a long tournament. Take a day off to go sightseeing. Get outside, relax, see a play, go to the zoo, play ping-pong – anything fun will work. "What!" you say, "Not play bridge every possible minute?" It does take time to get used to the idea, however I guarantee it will help prevent BBO.

It's also fun to play in different events. You might try one or two days of open pairs, and maybe two knockout events. Book your knockouts with different teams. Variety is spice, and spice helps prevent, you guessed it, BBO.

There's Hope
I genuinely hope this article is not for you, but if it strikes a chord, the good news is, BBO is not incurable. I got over my case quite quickly.

"If winter comes, can spring be far behind?" – *Percy Bysshe Shelley.*

* * *

WHAT ABOUT THOSE PROS?

"To be a winner, work with winners." – Warren Buffett.

Many beginners wonder about those mysterious pros. Do they really do you any good? How much does it cost to play with a pro? To take lessons from a pro? Are local pros truly pros?

First of all, there are many excellent players who give personal or group lessons. They may not be national experts, but are still players of stature, who have experience and knowledge, and who can benefit your game. They will give you "insider tips," pass along information not found in bridge books, and help you find, and correct, your blind spots. They will get rid of your bad habits and help you create good ones. When you take lessons from a local pro you can broaden and improve your game a lot faster than if left to your own devices.

Is this for you? It depends on your goals and ambitions. Have you been bit hard by the bridge bug? Are you anxious to improve … and *now*? Have you taken beginning lessons? Perhaps intermediate lessons? Have you read a few books? Do you have a steady partner who wants to participate in a learning adventure? To maximize the results and make it worthwhile to engage a pro, these first basic steps lay a good foundation. Without them, progress takes longer, and you pay more.

When you decide to approach a pro for help, do your research. Choose a pro as carefully as you would a partner. Masterpoints and flash are not the only criteria. You want to consider compatibility, personality, and style. Is the pro both a good player and a good instructor? Will the pro use your convention card? You don't want to be pressured to try an abundance of new

conventions if your main goal is to improve
your basic game.

I recommend you watch the pro play;
observe how he treats his partners, see what
his temperament is. Find out who his clients
are and get their input. It's good policy to
check a person's credentials before investing
too much time and money. Which reminds me, you
might want to inquire into his rates as well.

I recall playing with two pros who had
decidedly different approaches. One was a bit
hyper and quite focused on winning; patience
was not his long suit. I got a lot of good
information, but playing with him was
debilitating. I was fast losing my self-
esteem, and decided it was not worth it. My
second pro was very relaxed, praised me when I
made a good bid or play, and made me want to do
better just to please him. We had good
results, I learned a lot, and didn't mind at
all paying for the pleasure. He made me feel I
was fully capable of doing well.

Alternatives
        Don't be afraid to approach a player in
your local club as a mentor. There are many
good bridge players who can help improve your
game who wouldn't think of charging you a dime.
Simply ask one if he would be willing to help
you advance by playing with you once a week.
Let him know how much you admire his game, and
that your sources report he is not only a
wonderful player, but congenial as well.
Bridge players love flattery.

I myself worked with a beginner for over
a year and got great satisfaction watching her
game improve dramatically. The real bonus was
that I also acquired a lifelong friend.

Another alternative is to take lessons
from an ACBL Certified Teacher. Each teacher

134

has taken a 10-hour interactive course offered only at NABCs and Regionals. Instructors' names are available at your local club or can be accessed on-line at www.acbl.org. Rates are set independently. A certified teacher in our area charges $15/group and $25/private lessons. You get a bargain.

Group vs Individual Lessons

Life is full of trade-offs. Private lessons are more in-depth and tailored to your individual circumstances. They are also more expensive.

My partner and I took private lessons from a pro, and *wow* - what an eye-opener. We had been under the mistaken impression we pretty much knew it all. Our bridge egos were quickly deflated. We found out we had quite a way to go after all.

Our pro also gave group lessons. After a few months of intense, and necessary, individual bridge therapy, we were ready to switch. The group was a lot of fun, more social, and we still kept on learning. The pro set up tables and had the students bid and play. He supervised and gave commentary. The rate was $25/person, cheaper than our private lessons at $50/each.

National Pros

If you have an abundance of funds, you may have the itch to play with a Big Name. You set the stage via study, lessons from local experts, and a lot of practice. You want, perhaps, to get your Life Master's.

Big names charge big money. They restrict play with clients to Regionals and Nationals. They generally do not book a client for fewer than two days. In addition to fees you are expected to pay your pro's expenses and entries, and buy dinner. It ain't cheap. But

there is the glory, and hopefully the
masterpoints. The masterpoints, however, are
not guaranteed.

The Playing Arena

Club Games/Sectionals: The club (or a
local sectional) is an excellent place to play
with your mentor. The environment is familiar,
the atmosphere relaxed, and the field includes
friends and acquaintances. At a sectional you
may offer, as a courtesy, to buy your mentor's
entry fee.

Since the points available at a club game
are fewer compared to a tournament, I prefer
not to pay the $50/75 most local pros charge to
play at a club.

Sectionals/Regionals: These are the
events for which you ask a pro to reserve you a
spot. The pro will give you good advice as to
choice of games. I would believe him. Be sure
to ask his/her fee, because it will undoubtedly
be more than the fee you pay for lessons. You
don't want to be surprised. I have been quoted
$100/session for a Sectional and $200/session
for a Regional, but don't rely on these
figures. Fees can vary considerably from pro
to pro.

Bracketed Knockouts: If there is one
event made to play with a pro, this is it. If
you find a pro who doesn't have tens of
thousands of masterpoints, and there are many
such qualified players out there, you can play
in a moderate bracket and have a great chance
of doing well. Another advantage is that your
teammates will share the fee. This event is
especially attractive if you and your teammates
have been taking group lessons from the pro,
and thus are on the same page and play at the
same level. You definitely get more for your
money with this setup.

Online Pros

If you play online using a program like *OKBridge* you see many "experts" advertising to play-for-pay. You have a significant advantage with this format. You can, as a kibitzer, observe the pro in action for as long and as often as you like, without even leaving your own home. You will form an impression of his style and ability in no time. Via email you can easily get a quote for his fee. I have been quoted from $30/hour to $75/hour by online pros. Good pros will also let you know what to expect from them and offer to answer any initial questions. Most prefer to play in the "mini tournaments," since the hands are recorded and thus available for analysis after the game. Also, you can earn masterpoints in the mini's. Again, don't be led astray by the points or the rating a pro has. Take time to observe several candidates and go with the one you feel best suits you as an individual. Many online pros offer one free session, which is most helpful. You then get an even better sense of whether your choice was the right one.

Of course, life is full of trade-offs. Many on-line pros do not live in your area, and won't be able to play with you in live games or tournaments. They can, however, give you meaningful input and help improve your game exponentially in a very convenient setting.

Note - be cautious. I played with one on-line expert who was particularly in-depth. We got along fine during the game, and I learned a lot. However, after the game, part of the lesson plan was to go over the hands by phone. This man could talk, and talk, and talk. By the time we were through I had rung up at least 2 hours of fees and was brain dead. I had to terminate that relationship quickly.

Is there a Stigma?

We all hear gripes about players who get

their points playing with pros. This seems like sour grapes to me. We hire pros in other walks of life – CPAs, architects, plumbers. We could do these jobs ourselves, but might not be happy with the results. Playing with a pro is a cooperative effort. You must learn quickly, be alert, and hold up your end; even a pro can't create a win alone. Then too, you must play in whichever strata or bracket matches your pro's points, and he will usually be an "A" player. This can be challenging.

Don't listen to grapevine gossip. Do what you want to do to get the result you want. You aren't going to play with a pro the rest of your life (unless you marry one). You will soon move on to a regular partnership, using your new-found knowledge to be an effective partner.

In Summary
It is fun to play with, and take lessons from, a pro. I personally found it to be vitally helpful. It took me to a new level. It has been 5 years since then, and I am ready to seek out another expert for more fine-tuning. I strongly recommend it.

Just be sure to get the expert who is right for you. Remember, you are not locked in. You did not say "I do" to this expert. You can discontinue his/her services at any time and engage someone else. If it's not fun, you have the wrong person.

Whatever you decide, bridge pro, mentor, or simply to work one-on-one with your partner, you have found a great hobby. It is a universal pastime that keeps on going, is never boring, and brings constant adventure. Enjoy it to the fullest.

"Come my friends, 'tis not too late to seek a newer world." – Tennyson.

* * *

ARMCHAIR BRIDGE
Playing Electronically Around the World

"It is not down in any map; true places never are." - Herman Melville.

Playing on-line is a thrill. There is a whole new bridge world out there. You can play any time of the day or night - dressed for work or ready for bed, it doesn't matter. You can play with someone in San Francisco, London, Madrid, Toronto - the globe awaits. You can play with your favorite partner right down the street and earn masterpoints at the same time. How could a bridge fan ask for more?

The Sites

You can "Google" on-line bridge and find numerous available sites. Some are better than others. If you want to play for fun and practice and don't care about accumulating masterpoints, pick a site that looks good and try it out. Experiment. You'll soon find the one which suits you best. Many are free.

If you want to play for masterpoints, there are three official sites which offer that option. My favorite is *OKBridge*. This is a subscription site which is worth the fee. It is tightly run, well organized, beautifully laid out, and requires that members adhere to proper procedure and behavior. It has great customer service. The standard membership is $99/year with an additional $49/year if you want to play in the mini-tournaments which offer masterpoints. The "minis" are a series of 6 matches, 2 boards each, and take 60-70 minutes.

BridgeBase also offers 12-board masterpoint matches for $1.00 each. The basic program is free.

Swan Games has three ACBL tournaments per day that issue masterpoints; some are 12-board games and some 16-board games. You can purchase tickets for $.50/ticket or an unlimited monthly pass for $10.95.

Any site you visit has instructions which direct you through the process. It's helpful if you know someone who plays on-line and will act as an escort your first few times. If it gets tricky, message to the other players that you are new, a first-time user, and they will be kind and understanding. Usually.

The Arena

Of course there are pitfalls. Not every player you pick up, or who asks you for a game, is going to play your nice comfortable convention card. They may not have the personality of your comfortable steady partner (for some this may be an advantage). They may have a different style, be more aggressive or more conservative; they may play versions of various conventions which differ from your usual agreements. Right away you know you have been presented with a great learning opportunity.

The Rules

One of the first things to do upon venturing into bridge cyberspace is to learn the rules. Good manners are the key.

If you want to play at an open table, it is good etiquette to ask if you can join; don't immediately jump into a seat. The table "manager" may bump you right back out. It helps insure your acceptance if you choose a table where players have ratings which match your own range. (Ratings are percentage allocations assigned to players by the bridge program, based on the player's results. Ratings are reevaluated and changed each week.)

Greet the players at the table, and ask your partner if he/she can play your card. (Note: When you first join you will complete a personal "profile," which briefly outlines the systems and conventions you prefer to use.) Be prepared to mix and match; your partner will agree to play some of your card, and you in turn agree to play some of his. This is the time to ask more detailed systemic questions not outlined on your respective profiles.

When your partner is declarer, message "glp" - good luck partner. When you are declarer and dummy comes down, message "typ" - thank you partner. (For further translation of on-line abbreviations see "On-Line Lingo" at the end of this article.)

While playing, give no lessons, make no criticisms. This will avoid a bad reputation which would leave you hard pressed to find a partner. Mark time and suffer silently. You will soon come upon a player who likes most of your card and with whom you are in sync. Then the waiting will have been worth the while. Make appointments to play when you are both available so you can each have a pleasant game. If you check the "Add to Friends List" section of your partner's profile, his name will be highlighted when he comes on-line and you will hear a pleasant "ding".

On-line play often leads to off-line friendships and pairing up at tournaments. A player my partner and I met on-line invited us to stay at her home during a Regional in her neighboring home state. She was a true Southern hostess, and gave us a grand tour of her city's highlights. We also enjoyed the mint juleps.

There is a group of on-line players who, although most live in different states, get together once a year at a Regional. They trade stories, socialize, and of course (what else) play bridge.

Many players enjoy the "mini-tournaments," a series of six rounds, two boards each. Playing in these with your regular partner can be particularly helpful. Mini's provide a great practice tool, as hands are recorded. If you have a problem on a particular hand and want to discuss it later, you can print that hand out on-site as you play. After the tournament, results are emailed to you within 15 minutes. You can compare your results with the rest of the field, and analyze your bidding, play and defense quickly and easily. If your steady partner isn't on hand, a "Partnership Desk" is available. You may ask a member to play; others can ask you to play. If you decline, do so tactfully. Something like "Sorry, can't, but thanks for asking," is nice.

Once you arrange a partnership, you and your partner go to the tournament site, and your partner clicks on your name. A pop-up appears on the screen. You click "yes" to validate acceptance. Be aware there are people already at the site who do not have partners (they are not following standard procedure). They may ask you to play a second before your partner puts in his request. Be sure you are accepting an invitation from the *correct partner*. Many times a player clicks "yes" without looking, and ends up with the wrong partner in the tournament. Not a good feeling. The director doesn't like it either.

When the tournament begins, you need to announce your main system briefly at the beginning of each round. For example, "2/1, standard, Capp, o/e, 1430" would be common. For more details the opponets look at your stats, or your posted convention card. (Most on-line systems provide a way to complete and post a convention card).

If a misunderstanding comes up during bidding or play wait to inquire until *after the hand is over*. Then you and your partner can iron it out.

Go Global
You will expand your availability as well as your choice of partners if you become familiar with the most popularly used conventions.

When you check out the "Player Information" section of each member's "Profile" you will notice certain conventions or their variations are played almost universally. Although you may not know these conventions, it is worth your while to look them up, or ask an expert for details. This way you recognize them, can defend against them, and when asked, play them yourself. This makes you a flexible and desirable partner.

Be Practical
Your ability to be a switch-hitter will come in handy. WHEN PLAYING WITH SOMEONE NEW, USE THEIR CONVENTIONS. Do not be misled by a player's willingness to play your card. Regardless of intentions, if your partner is used to Capp, they will forget DONT. If they are used to 1430 they will forget 3014. If they use o/e, your standard signal will be misinterpreted at just the wrong time. Other areas of misunderstanding involve Drury, UDCA, 3/5 vs. 4th best leads, Bergen, and whether you use 2, 3 or 4 suit transfers over an opening 1NT. If your partner's list of conventions on his profile is not detailed, ask about these common areas of concern.

Keep a notepad by your computer and jot down reminders of your discussions with new partners on these points. Make special note of conventions or treatments that differ from your standard convention card.

Sometimes, no matter how careful you are, there will be adventures you could do without. I played on-line against a pickup pair who had never played together before. Both had Jacoby Transfers on their card. Right hand opponent opens 1NT, his partner bids 2H (transfer to spades), she passes. He corrects to 2S after the opponents double, and she bids 3H! Needless to say this was not a contract they wanted to be in. He messages her afterward that he thought they were playing transfers.

Silence.

We proceed. Another hand goes by, and sure enough, 1NT again by our otherwise mute opponent. After his lecture responder feels confident and again tries to transfer with 2D. Of course, his partner bids 3D. This time he passes, hoping for the best. The best did not happen. But partner, he bleats, you have transfers on your card.

Nothing.

By now we are all wondering who made up her card. Her poor partner is desperately hoping that she will not have another 1NT opener. But against all odds, or perhaps this particular day it was with the odds, she once more opens 1NT. This time her partner decides to forget all about transfers and bid 2H, his real suit. Of all times, she finally comes alive, and bids 2S. The poor man just couldn't take it, claimed an emergency, and left the table, thanking his partner for the game (he was following at least one of the rules).

Some days, some partners, you have to expect the unexpected. I would not be surprised if he marked his private diary (see below) "avoid at all costs".

Be Smart

If you start to open your mouth, *keep your fingers off the keys*. It is best to make no comments or suggestions, no matter how valid, when you play with a new partner. Your helpful hints are not always kindly received, and may result in your getting a reputation as one who likes to give "lessons". This is as socially unacceptable as bad breath. You may however communicate such niceties as "wdp" (well done partner), "great bid," "wow," etc. If your partner has the courage to say "sorry" after a big goof, restrain yourself with an "np" (no problem). Your opponents will be silently sympathetic and you will be seen as a very tactful partner.

Embarrassing Moments

It is also a good idea to send your message to the right person. During play you are able to privately message both opponents at the same time, or send a message to only one opponent. This is generally used to explain an alerted bid or a coded lead. Sometimes, however, you can't restrain yourself from sending personal messages. You may feel sympathy for an opponent whose partner is always berating him. When you message "what a grump" to the wrong opponent it can be a tad bit awkward.

I remember a pair at a tourney who had just arrived for the next round. One of the pair was complaining about an opponent from the previous round who was obnoxious. The other of the pair kept asking her partner whether or not they were playing a specific convention; her partner never answered. I messaged (I thought) the opponent who was asking about the convention. I said, "He must be a man." (I find men sometimes ignore questions.)

However, I had actually messaged her partner. Realizing my mistake, I then messaged the correct opponent, hoping her partner would disappear. Miraculously, the complainer thought I meant his obnoxious opponent from the last round must have been a man. Our two current opponents got together and both thought we were very clever with our banter about men. Whew. A bullet dodged. However, I am very careful now about checking at least twice that I am messaging the correct person.

Private Diary

It is useful to keep your own private on-line commentary on casual partnerships. There is a place for "Comments" on each player's Profile (at least on *OK Bridge*). I use this space for a brief description of my experience with a player. I may note "steady," "not advanced," "great" or "no-no-no". This is helpful since I may not remember the player a few weeks later when asked to play again. I look at the comment and know whether I want to accept or decline the invitation.

Help Keep Players Honest

Also in the Profile section is a place to "complain". I do not hesitate to use this section if I feel it will help educate the offending player. General areas of concern are rudeness, non-alerts, being unresponsive to questions, or making an unsubstantiated or premature claim.

Enjoy

If you do decide to play on-line, there is only one warning. It can be soooooooooo addictive. I do not let myself go on-line unless I have completed half of my chores for the day. Or I promise myself to do those chores after one quick game … maybe do them tomorrow?

In any event, electronic bridge expands your horizons while providing pleasurable entertainment. It is a great tool for partnerships and provides the opportunity to practice more often than if you were limited to "live" games only. It can't take the place of person-to-person bridge, seeing your friends, feeling that table presence. But it isn't a bad substitute.

"If you never did, you should. These things are fun, and fun is good." - Dr.Seuss.

On-Line Lingo:
brb = be right back
Capp = Cappelletti
fofl = falling on floor laughing
lol = laughing out loud
np = no problem
o/e = odd/even
typ = thank you partner
UDCA = upside-down count and attitude
vwdp = very well done partner
wdp = well done partner
wdo = well done opponents

* * *

THE GOOD OLD DAYS
A Memoir

"You cannot step twice into the same river, for other waters are continually flowing on." –
Heraclitus.

We all, young and old, love to reminisce about the good old days – even if they only go back as far as the high school prom. Unfortunately, high school is a microdot on my own dateline, which goes back to the Jurassic Age.

I do, however, remember the tender days of my initiation into the bridge world. It was an exciting, giddy time. I had been hooked by a noon-time rubber game, which soon became the highlight of my day. Being a bit skeptical, I didn't quite trust the information I was getting. I wanted "Just the facts, ma'am, just the facts." So I ventured out to the local bridge club for lessons from Those Who Know.

The Universe was looking out for me. I landed in a huge, well-established club. Lessons, provided by experienced players, were readily available at every level. I gorged myself. When I just knew I was going to accumulate points right and left, I plunked myself into the middle of the beginner's section, feeling invincible. I wasn't. Fortunately, partners were guaranteed, so I kept plodding on.

I got the hang of it, and started getting little slips of paper showing the .03 points or so I had earned. I hoarded these trophies, until I had upwards of 100 of the beautiful things to send to ACBL. In those days there were no computers; everything was done by hand. Points were issued by directors, and handed to players. The players then had the

responsibility of mailing the points to
Headquarters. If you lost your documentation,
too bad. Those points were toast. I never
lost one of those precious sheets, believe me.

Soon I was whizzing along, thinking I was
King Kong. The little beginner's pool started
to bore me. I knew I wasn't quite ready for
the Open section (shudder), but had to try it.
I jumped right in. The director looked out for
me, and paired me with some nice intermediates.
Somehow I never seemed to get the same partner
twice ... One kind senior player brought me a
stack of old Bridge Bulletins, a hopeful look
on his face.

My doubts were confirmed, I wasn't quite
ready. But I stoically accepted looks of utter
disbelief. I welcomed all lessons. I listened
to the better players discuss hands and
bidding. That alone paid for the suffering and
ignominy. Soon players stopped running in the
opposite direction when I approached the
director for a partner. I gradually blended
what I had learned with reality, and the fickle
nature of the cards. I felt part of the Club.

I finally stumbled onto a benign mentor
who agreed to play with me once a week. My
game got better. I was advised to read
Watson's Play of the Hand, my first bridge
book. It brought further revelations. I was
here to stay.

My vision now expanded even more. I was
hearing about these "tournaments" that seemed
to sparkle and glitter. I decided to see what
they were all about. Keep in mind that in
those days there were no bracketed KO's, no
flighted events, no separation of A, B and C
players. You put on your boxing gloves and
duked it out. Neither was there any concept of
active ethics or zero tolerance - just a lot of
intolerance. There were no bidding boxes.

There was a constant low murmur in the playing area, which increased to a dull roar as players finished hands and boards. There was definitely a possibility that less than ethical players would overhear bids and comments, and use this information to their benefit. At the club level this was more or less contained, but at a large tournament it was almost impossible to police every player. Smoke filled the room. Even a gas mask was useless. Yes, tournaments were daunting.

The first step was to approach the partnership desk. Everyone always lied about their master points, to get a better partner. Of course the better partner was also lying about his master points. There was no Big Brother watching you back then. It was a wild and wooly free-for-all.
.
I remember one late game in San Francisco. An energetic senior had been up in the ballroom dancing the night away. He wasn't sure whether to play, with me, the only one left looking for a partner, or continue dancing. We played, and came in third, to my delight. I was a rank beginner then. He was probably astounded, but had been very tactful throughout. He didn't need zero tolerance or active ethics – being a gentleman was in his genes.

After the game, dedicated directors often spent hours scoring and correcting results, by hand, with "helpful" onlookers, thick as gnats, swirling around and peering over shoulders. More often than not the exasperated director would end up shooing everyone away, only to have them all return, one by one, within minutes. Many players simply came back the next morning to catch the results.

Soon, at both tournaments and club games, the smoking issue could no longer be ignored.

The Powers That Be were all doom and gloom. They just knew that bridge would fail, would disappear in a thin fog, if smoking were banned. They were sure smokers would leave forever, as they had threatened. Ha ha ha. Those smokers were addicted not only to cigarettes, but to bridge as well. Once restrictions began, a few smokers left – for maybe two weeks.

The first hesitant step taken was to create two sections, one smoking and one non-smoking. One could look across the room and see a black cloud hovering over the smokers. I didn't smoke, but my partner and I, after a few boring sessions, looked at one another, nodded, and headed over to the smoking section. All the better, more exciting players were there. As Friedrich Nietzsche says, "In Heaven, all the interesting people are missing".

This method did not last long. Soon the playing room was *entirely* smoke-free, with antsy players jumping up after each round and running out to puff away. Beware of opening the door – you would be enveloped in leftover smoke. Smoking was soon relegated to the bathrooms. Non-smokers developed strong bladders. Now, as you know, smoking must be done outside, or in your smoking room, if the hotel even offers one. Smokers now seem to be able to pace themselves, and have not jumped ship on us after all.

Yes, bridge has certainly changed from "way back when". Some of it is for the better. Some of it I wish had stayed the same. That's true of many things in life.

I love the cutting-edge, winner-take-all, bidding wars that now proliferate at club and tournament alike. There is more science, coupled with inventive creativity, which makes for an ever-changing, never boring game. New conventions, new tools, greater awareness of the potential of communication within our limited bridge vocabulary, all make for an exciting environment. I must admit, my beginning bridge lessons made Roth-Stone look like far-left radicals.

At the same time, I miss the unlimited open games, where one could play against the best of the best. We weren't in a hurry, points would come. Meanwhile we had a chance for a top against a national expert, which would give us a glory story to tell for many a day.

Although many old-timers complain they had to get their Life Master the hard way, I don't really think there is an easy way to become Life Master. There are a multitude of events now, and B and C can be separated from the A's. This helps. But bridge players are more savvy and sophisticated now, as well. This doesn't help. Some of the B players of today equate to yesterday's A players.

Yes, I reminisce often, with a soft sigh. Then I reflect on today and extol the current virtues. I hope that tomorrow will be even better so that today's beginners can look back on these times as the "good old days".

"'Old times' never come back and I suppose it's just as well. What comes back is a new morning every day in the year, and that's better." – *George E. Woodberry.*

***

REFERENCE MATERIAL

Andersen, Ron, Match Point Tactics,
    Shelbyville, KY, Devyn Press, 1981
Eber, Patty and Freeman, Mike, Have I Got a
    Story For You!,
    Louisville, KY, Devyn Press
Sanders, Carol and Tommy, Swiss Team Tactics,
    Shelbyville, KY, Devyn Press, 1981
Stewart, Frank, Article, Daily Bridge Calendar,
    Canada, Ashlar House, Inc., 2006
Wolff, Bobby, Article, Daily Bridge Calendar,
    Canada, Ashlar House, Inc., 2006

SUGGESTED READING

Instructional
Bergen, Marty, Better Slam Bidding with Bergen
Bergen, Marty, Negative Doubles
Bergen, Marty, Points Schmoints!
Lawrence, Mike, Complete Book on Balancing
Lawrence, Mike, Double!
Lawrence, Mike, Dynamic Defense
Lawrence, Mike, How to Read Your Opponents'
    Cards
Lawrence, Mike, Judgment at Bridge
Lawrence, Mike, Opening Leads
Lawrence, Mike, Overcalls
Root, Bill, How to Play a Bridge Hand
Root, Bill, How to Defend a Bridge Hand

Reference
Root, William and Pavlicek, Richard, Modern
    Bridge Conventions
Watson, Louis, The Play of the Hand at Bridge

For Fun
Mahmood, Zia, Bridge My Way
Mollo, Victor, You Need Never Lose at Bridge

You can find these and many more at Baron
Barclay Bridge Supply. You can request a
catalog at 1 800 274 2221.

INDEX

ORDER YOUR OWN COPY
SEND A GIFT COPY

Special Offer: Order *SECRETS* and receive a **free** subscription to Cathy Hunsberger's Bridge Unlimited Newsletter.

To Order *SECRETS* via email:

Amazon: www.amazon.com/books
Ebook copy: www.ebooksbridge.com

You may also request an autographed copy from the author at chunsberger@cox.net.

For your free newsletter, email Cathy at chunsberger@cox.net. Mention Special Offer No. 111. With two or more orders from Cathy, receive a 10% rebate. Mention Special Offer No. 112.

ORDER YOUR OWN COPY
SEND A GIFT COPY

Special Offer: Order *SECRETS* and receive a **free** subscription to Cathy Hunsberger's Bridge Unlimited Newsletter.

To Order *SECRETS* via email:

Amazon: www.amazon.com/books
Ebook copy: www.ebooksbridge.com

You may also request an autographed copy from the author at chunsberger@cox.net.

For your free newsletter, email Cathy at chunsberger@cox.net. Mention Special Offer No. 111. With two or more orders from Cathy, receive a 10% rebate. Mention Special Offer No. 112.

Breinigsville, PA USA
20 August 2010
243913BV00004B/3/P